AF228646

Dinosaur Jumbo

BOOKS OUT LOUD COLLECTION

Dinosaur Jumbo

by Grace Hansen

Welcome to BOOKS OUT LOUD!
This one-of-a-kind collection consists of twelve wildly popular Abdo Zoom titles, the bestselling classroom favorites. Get ready to feed your brain with the same amazing Abdo Read-to-Me experience kids know and love at school—and become a powerhouse reader anytime, anywhere.

Please scan the QR code on the back cover to link to the accompanying audio, or visit www.downpour.com/dinosaur-jumbo

Contents

Allosaurus

by Grace Hansen

Table of Contents

Allosaurus

Allosaurus lived in the late Jurassic period, about 150 million years ago.

Allosaurus were

theropods.

Habitat

Allosaurus lived in plains near rivers and lakes.

Body

Allosaurus could weigh nearly 3,000 pounds (1,360 kg). They could grow more than 30 feet (9.1 m) long. They were 15 to 17 feet (4.6 to 5.2 m) tall.

An allosaurus had a
thick, sturdy body. It
had a very long tail.

It had two powerful
legs and two short
arms. Each arm ended
in three long claws.

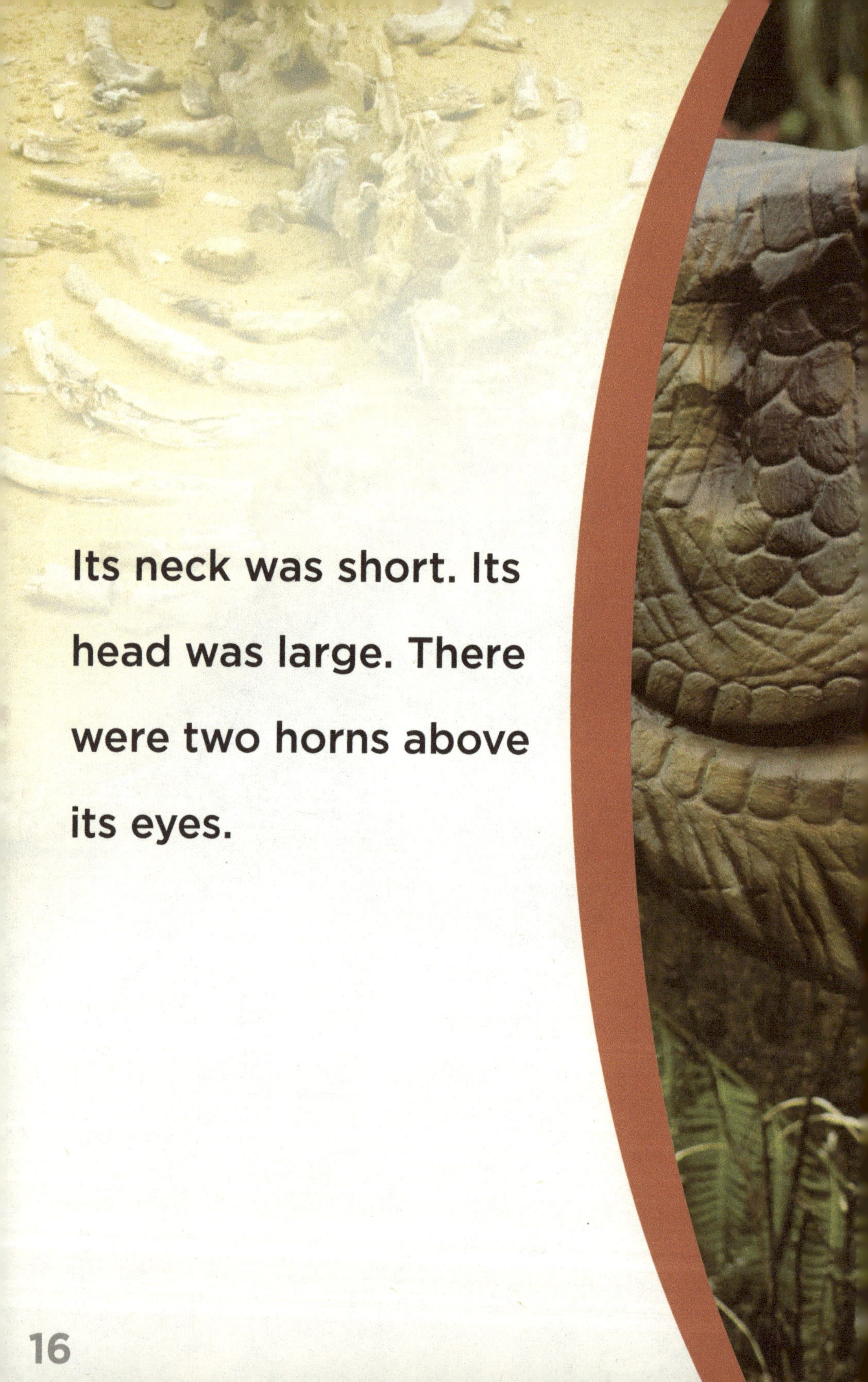

Its neck was short. Its head was large. There were two horns above its eyes.

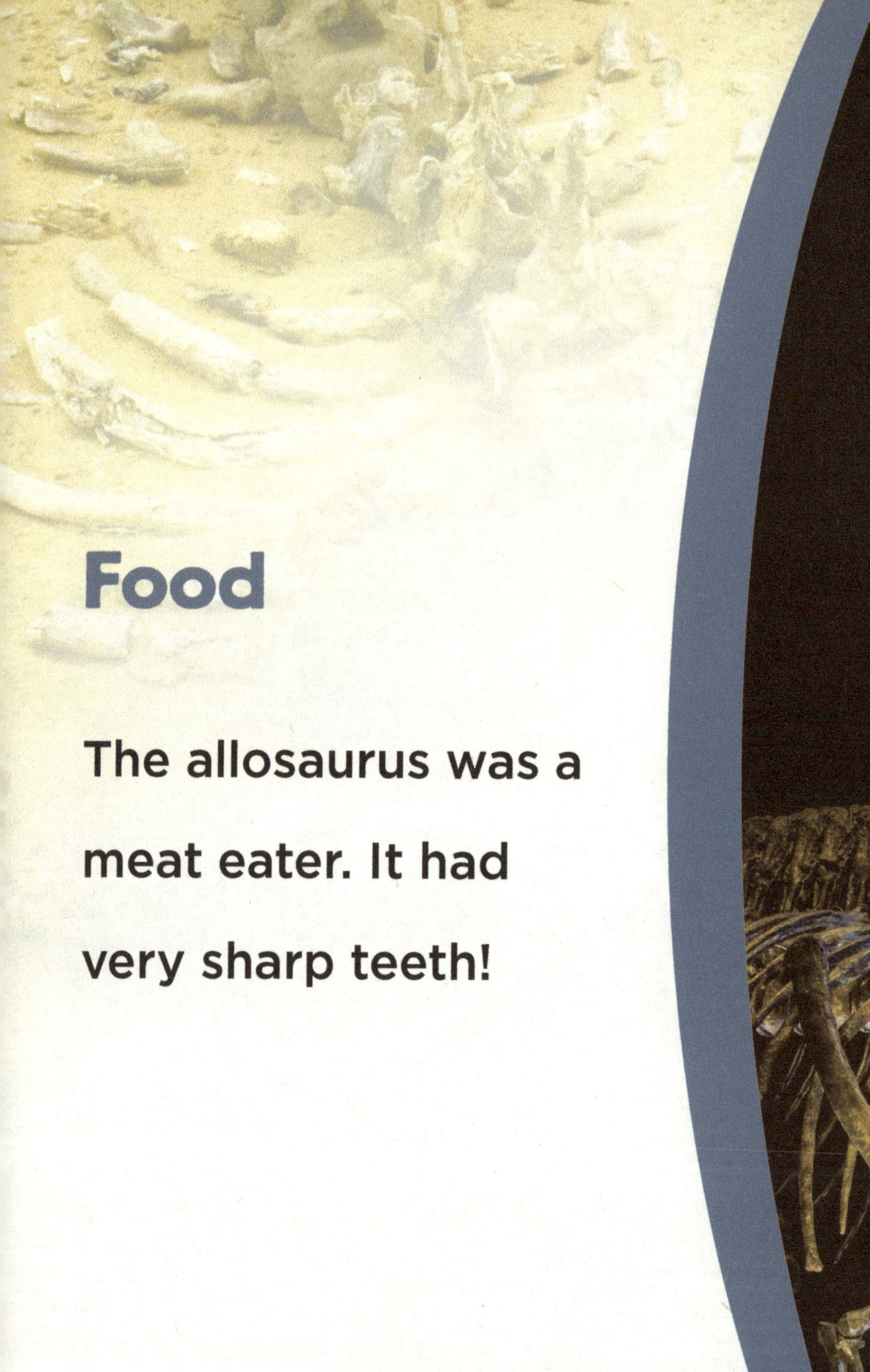

Food

The allosaurus was a meat eater. It had very sharp teeth!

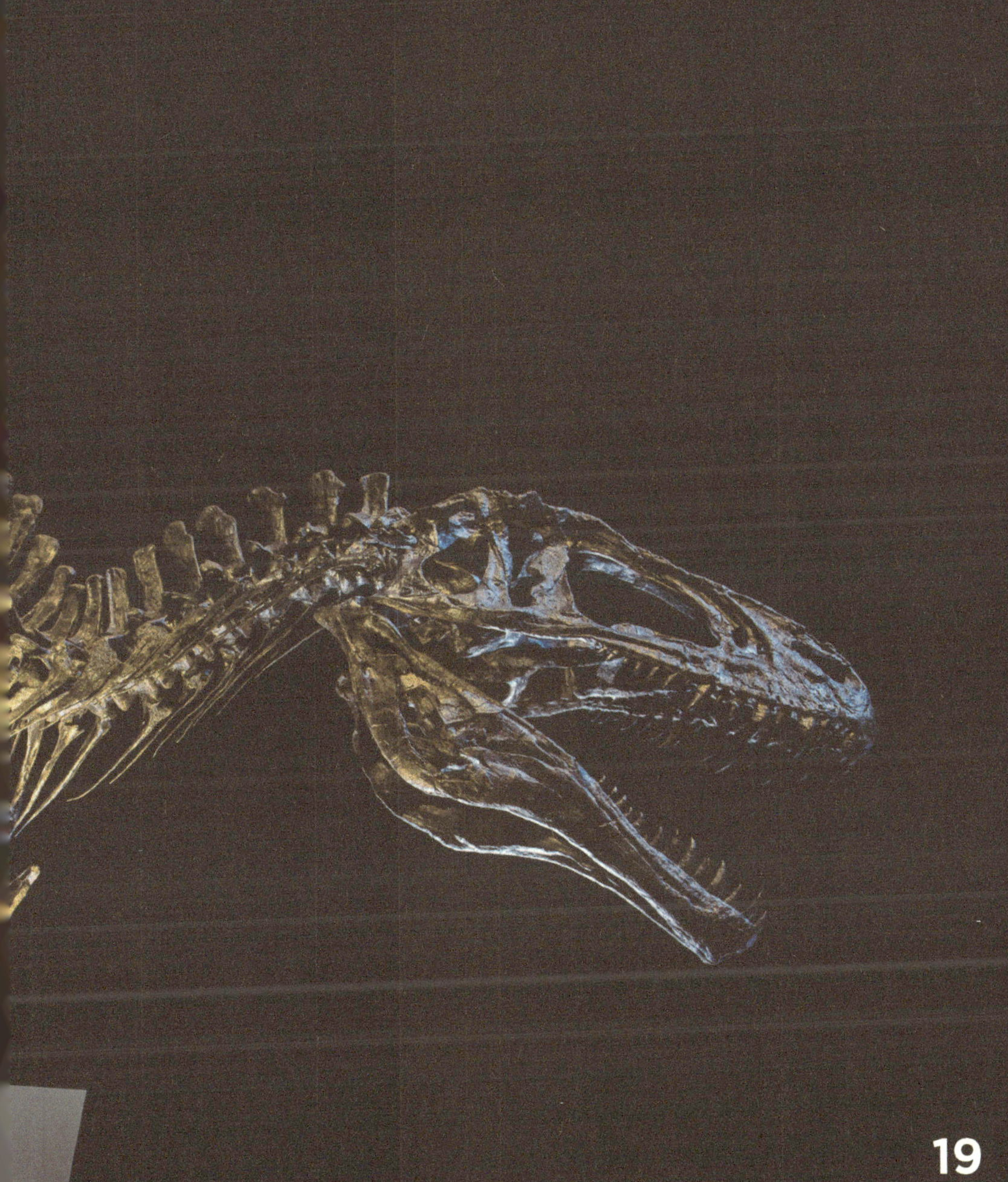

Fossils

Many Allosaurus fossils have been found in Utah. The most fossils were uncovered in Wyoming and Colorado.

Wyoming
Utah
Colorado

More Facts

- By age 15, Allosaurus had grown to their full adult size. Scientists think that Allosaurus could have lived 25 to 30 years.

- There are three main Allosaurus species known to scientists. The biggest difference between species is size.

- Paleontologists have found Allosaurus fossils with injuries the same shape and size as the tail spikes of Stegasaurus.

Glossary

fossil – the remains, impression, or trace of something that lived long ago, as a skeleton, footprint, etc.

Jurassic period – named after the Jura Mountains where rocks of this age were first found, this time period saw many lush plants, large plant-eating dinosaurs, and smaller meat-eating dinosaurs.

paleontologist – a scientist who studies fossils.

species – a group of animals that look alike, share many characteristics, and can produce young together.

theropod – a meat-eating dinosaur that comes in many sizes and usually has small forelimbs.

Ankylosaurus

by Grace Hansen

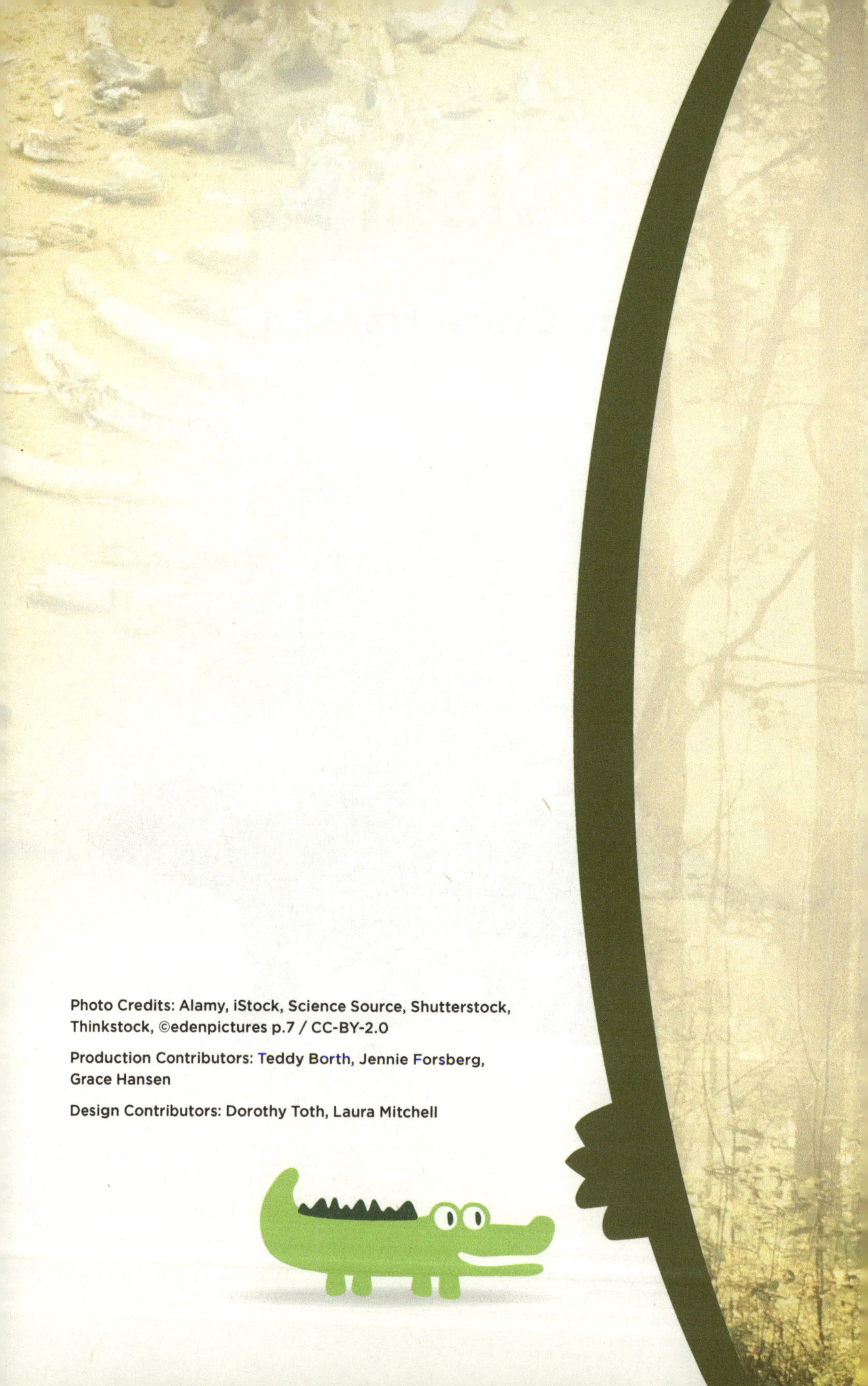

Table of Contents

Ankylosaurus

Ankylosaurus lived in the late Cretaceous period, around 70 million years ago. North America looked very different then. A shallow sea covered much of the land.

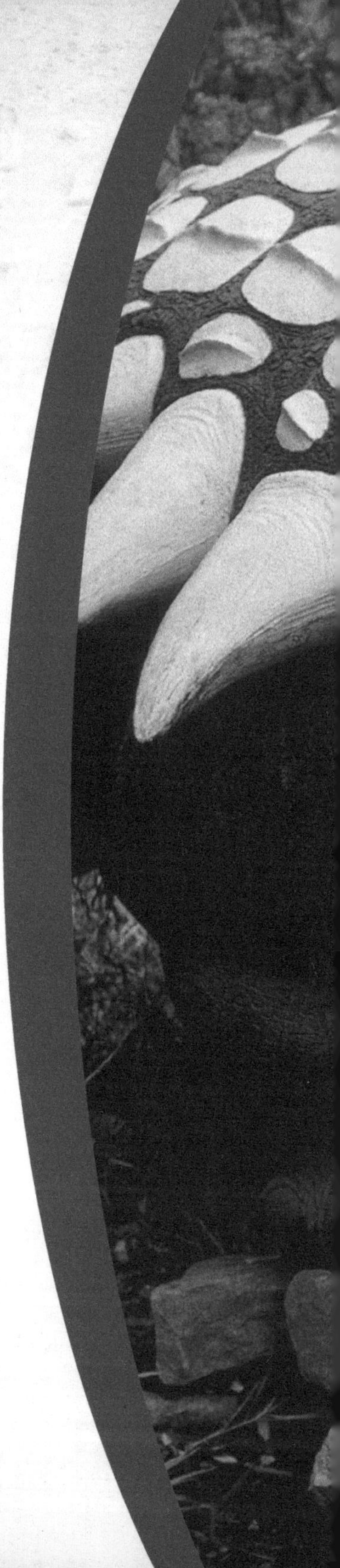

There were several

Ankylosaurus species.

But all had very similar

characteristics.

Habitat

Ankylosaurus lived in coastal areas. It was hot and humid. Many plants grew there.

Body

Ankylosaurus was a massive dinosaur! It could weigh up to 12,000 pounds (5,443 kg). It was around 20 feet (6.1 m) long and 6 feet (1.8 m) tall.

Ankylosaurus
stood on four
legs. Their bodies
were tough and
armored.

This dinosaur had a long and strong tail. It ended in a club. The club was probably used for defense.

Food

Ankylosaurus ate
low-lying plants.
They had leaf-shaped
teeth and a beak.
These worked well for
plucking plants.

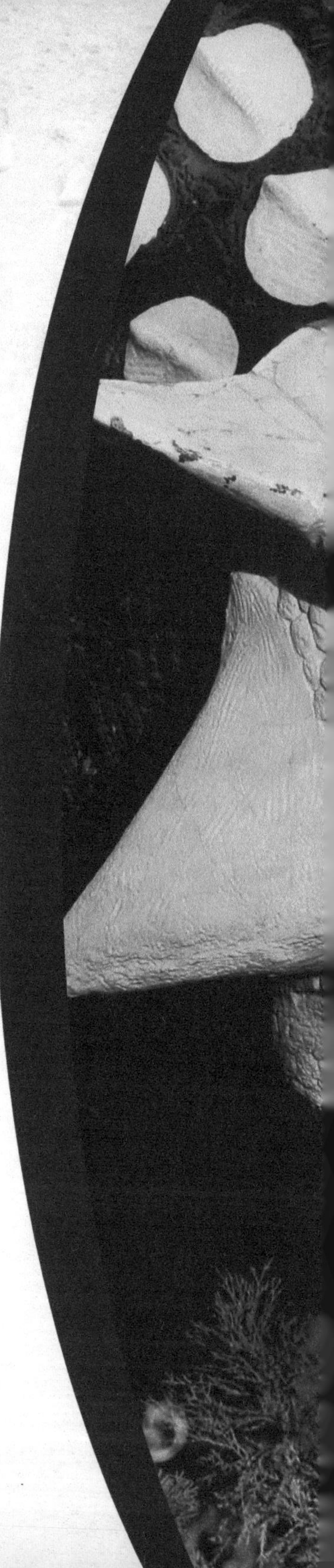

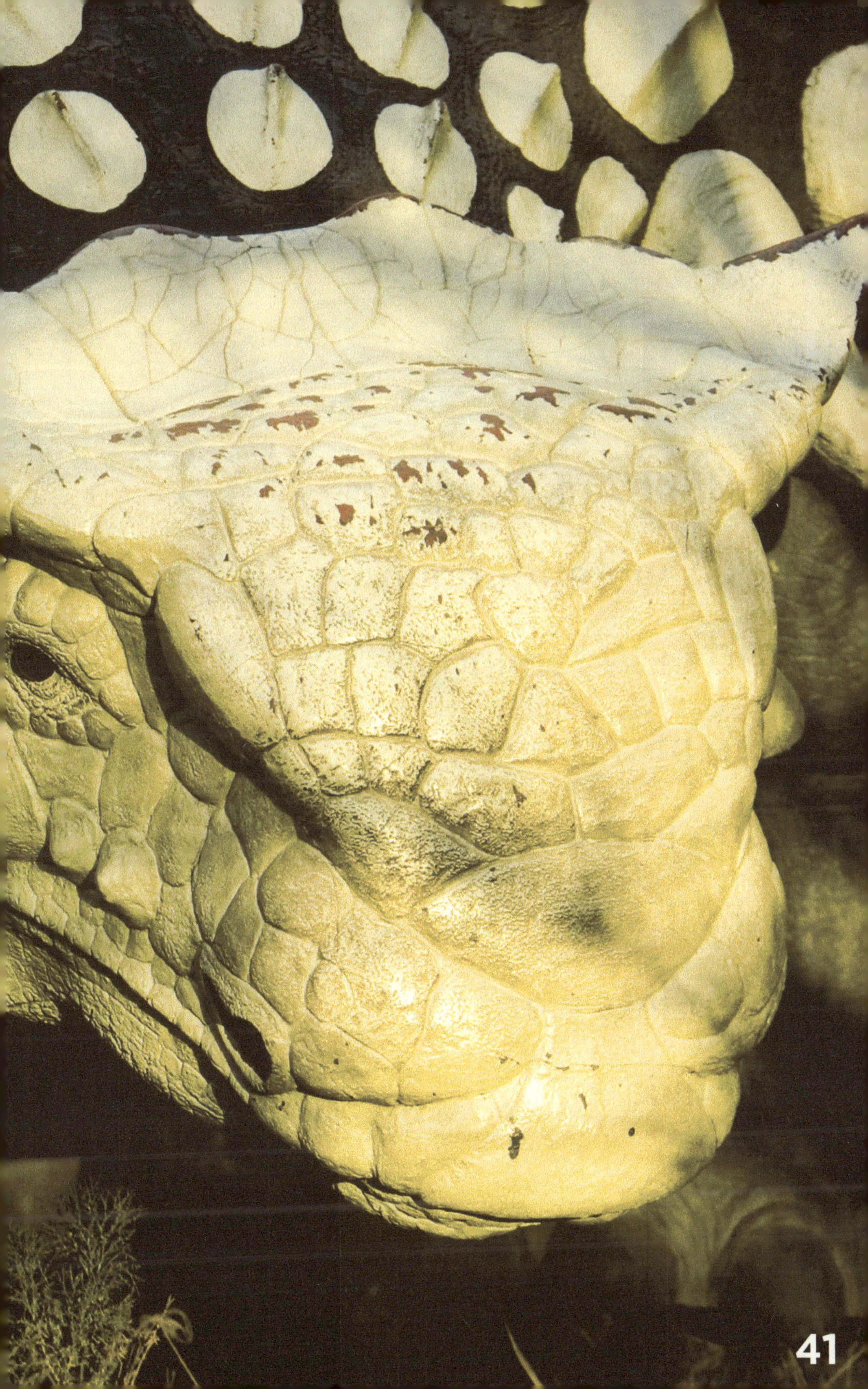

Fossils

The first Ankylosaurus fossils were found in 1900 in Wyoming. More have been found in Montana and Alberta, Canada. Footprints were found in Bolivia in 1996.

Montana
Wyoming

No full skeleton has been found yet. But two nearly complete ones have been uncovered. They have allowed us to learn about this awesome dinosaur!

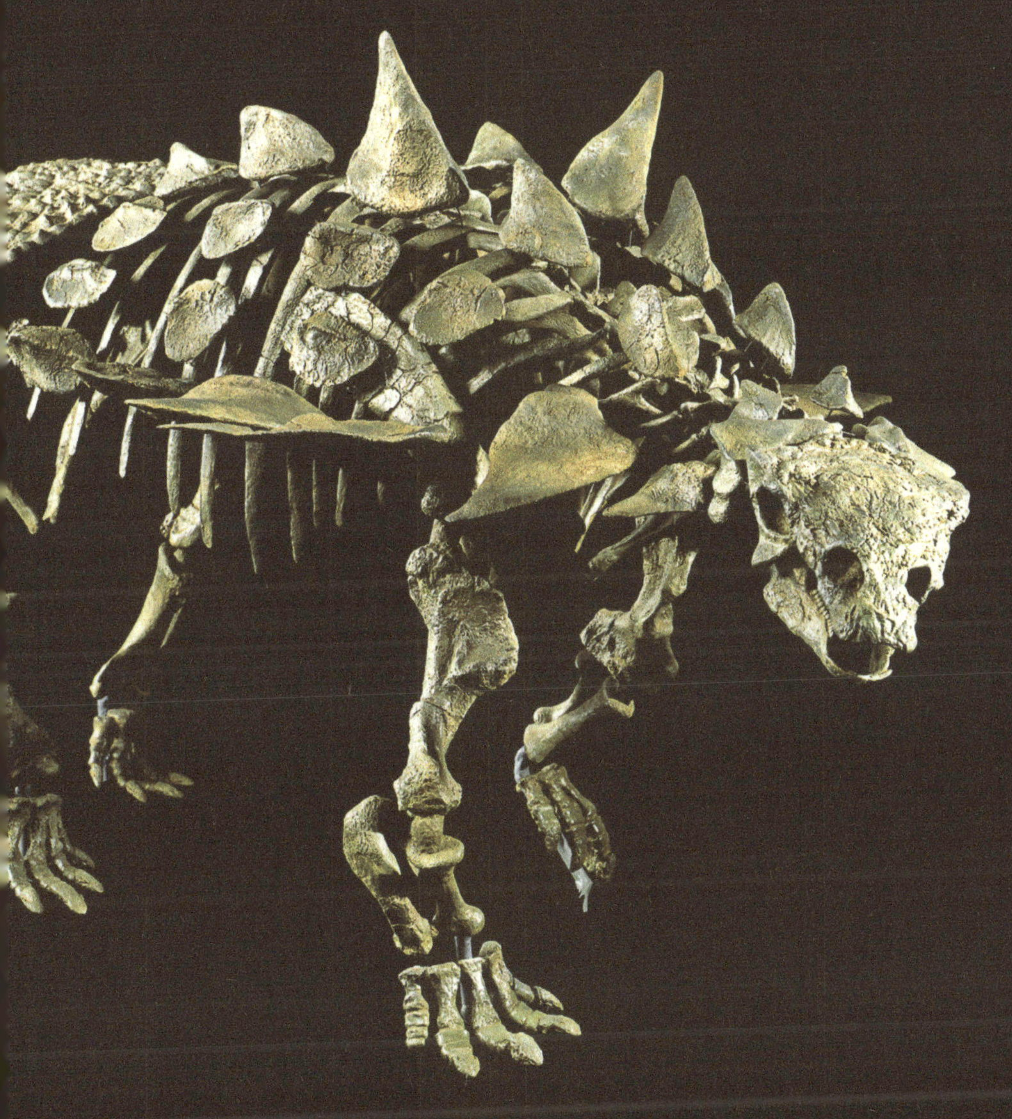

More Facts

- Ankylosaurus means "fused lizard." This refers to the fused bones in its skull and other parts of its body.

- These dinosaurs were protected by bony plates, which probably helped them survive attacks.

- Fossil scientists, called paleontologists, believe that Ankylosaurus used their powerful tails to break the bones of other dinosaurs.

Glossary

armored – protected by a hard material.

characteristic – a certain feature that serves to identify a thing.

Cretaceous period – rocks from the Cretaceous period often show early insects and the first flowering plants. The end of the Cretaceous period, about 65 million years ago, brought the mass extinction of dinosaurs.

fossils – the remains, impression, or trace of something that lived long ago, as a skeleton, footprint, etc.

species – a group of animals that look alike, share many characteristics, and can produce young together.

Diplodocus

by Grace Hansen

Table of Contents

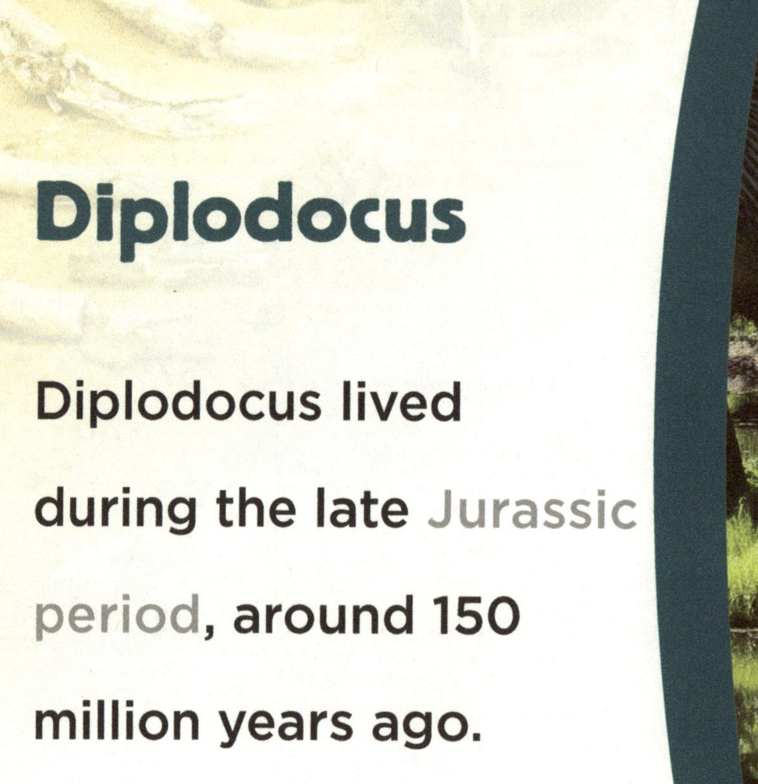

Diplodocus

Diplodocus lived during the late Jurassic period, around 150 million years ago.

Diplodocus were

sauropods.

Sauropods were

large plant eaters.

Habitat

Diplodocus lived in grasslands on the edges of forests. Rivers and lakes were nearby.

Body

A Diplodocus weighed more than 20,000 pounds (9,072 kg). It could grow more than 80 feet (24.4 m) long.

Its head, neck, and tail made up about 80% of its length. Four strong legs supported this dinosaur's very long body.

60%
20%
100%

Its head was small in comparison to the dinosaur's body. The mouth held 40 peg-shaped teeth. Its teeth tilted forward just a bit.

Food

Diplodocus ate plants. They stripped branches of their leaves. They had to eat a lot due to their huge size.

Diplodocus probably held their heads low. They may have reared onto their back legs to eat from treetops. But it was likely easier for them to eat from low plants.

Fossils

The first Diplodocus fossils were found in 1877. They were uncovered in Morrison, Colorado. Since then, many more remains have been found.

Colorado

More Facts

- Fossil hunters Earl Douglas and Samuel W. Williston were the first to uncover Diplodocus fossils in 1877.

- Othniel C. Marsh, a fossil scientist, named Diplodocus in 1878. He used the Greek words "diplos" (meaning "double") and "dokos" (meaning "beam").

- A Diplodocus may have fought other dinosaurs with its tail, which it could use like a whip.

Glossary

fossils – the remains, impression, or trace of something that lived long ago, as a skeleton, footprint, etc.

Jurassic period – named after the Jura Mountains where rocks of this age were first found, this time period saw many lush plants, large plant-eating dinosaurs, and smaller meat-eating dinosaurs.

sauropod – a very large plant-eating dinosaur that stood on four long legs and had a long neck and tail, and a small head.

Iguanodon

by Grace Hansen

Table of Contents

Iguanodon

Iguanodon lived during the early Cretaceous period. That was around 125 million years ago.

Iguanodon was

an ornithopod.

It ate plants.

Body

Iguanodon could grow up to 16 feet (4.9 m) tall. It weighed around 10,000 pounds (4,536 kg)!

Iguanodon had thick
hind legs. It had short,
skinny arms.

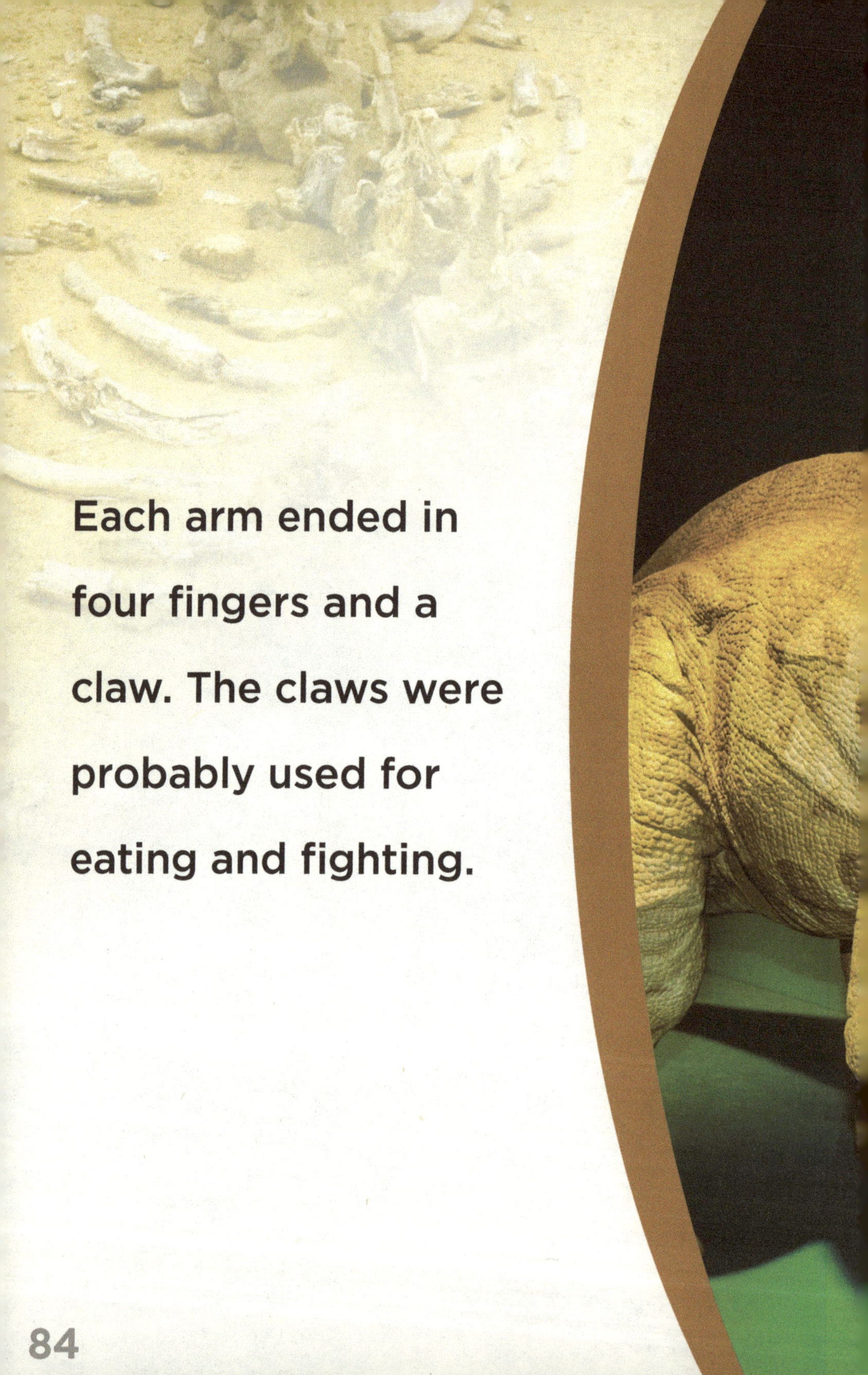

Each arm ended in four fingers and a claw. The claws were probably used for eating and fighting.

Iguanodon walked on all four limbs. It may have run on its back legs. It used its long tail for balance.

Iguanodon had
a small head. It
plucked leaves with
its beak. The back
of its mouth was full
of teeth. Iguanodon
was very good at
chewing its food.

Climate & Food

The **climate** was very warm and wet when Iguanodon was alive. There were lots of plants for Iguanodon to eat.

Fossils

Iguanodon fossils have been found around the world. The first were found in 1822 in England. More fossils have been found in Europe, Africa, and North America.

North America

More Facts

- Iguanodon means "iguana-like teeth." The first fossils found had teeth that look like an iguana's, except much larger.

- Preserved footprints found in southern England showed that these dinosaurs may have traveled in groups.

- Iguanodon's unique thumb spikes were thought to be horns that grew from the dinosaur's head. Fossil scientists learned where the spikes went when they found more complete remains in the 1870s.

Glossary

balance – an even distribution of weight to remain upright.

beak – the hard, pointed part of some dinosaurs' mouths.

climate – the weather in an area for a long period of time.

Cretaceous period – rocks from the Cretaceous period often show early insects and the first flowering plants. The end of the Cretaceous period, about 65 million years ago, brought the mass extinction of dinosaurs.

fossil – the remains, impression, or trace of something that lived long ago, as a skeleton, footprint, etc.

ornithopod – a plant-eating dinosaur that often walked or ran on its hind legs.

Spinosaurus

by Grace Hansen

Table of Contents

Spinosaurus

Spinosaurus lived in the Cretaceous period. That was about 95 million years ago.

Spinosaurus was

a theropod. It

ate meat.

Body

Spinosaurus was the largest meat-eating dinosaur. It grew more than 50 feet (15.24 m) long! It could weigh more than 16,000 pounds (7,257.5 kg).

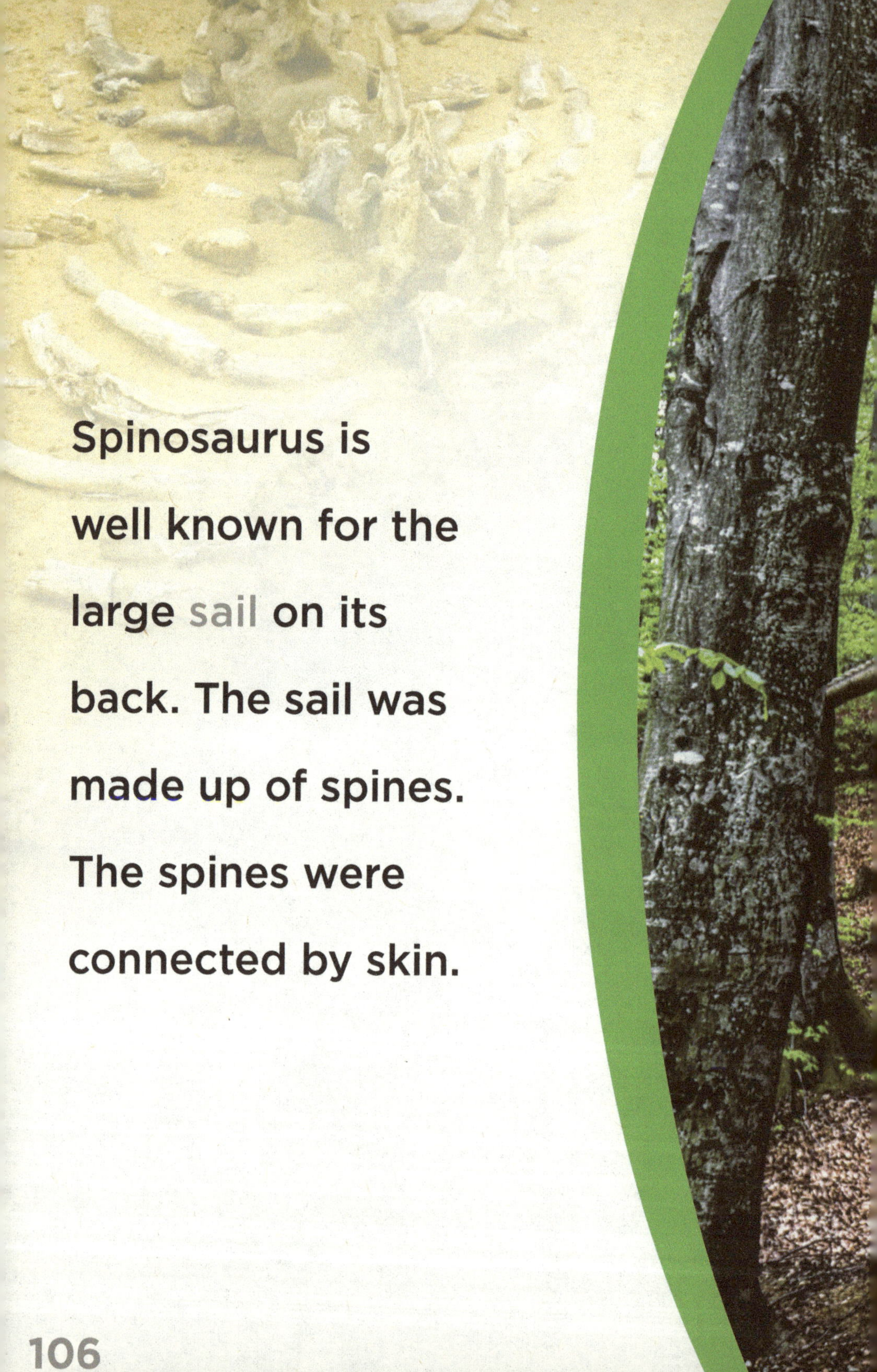

Spinosaurus is well known for the large sail on its back. The sail was made up of spines. The spines were connected by skin.

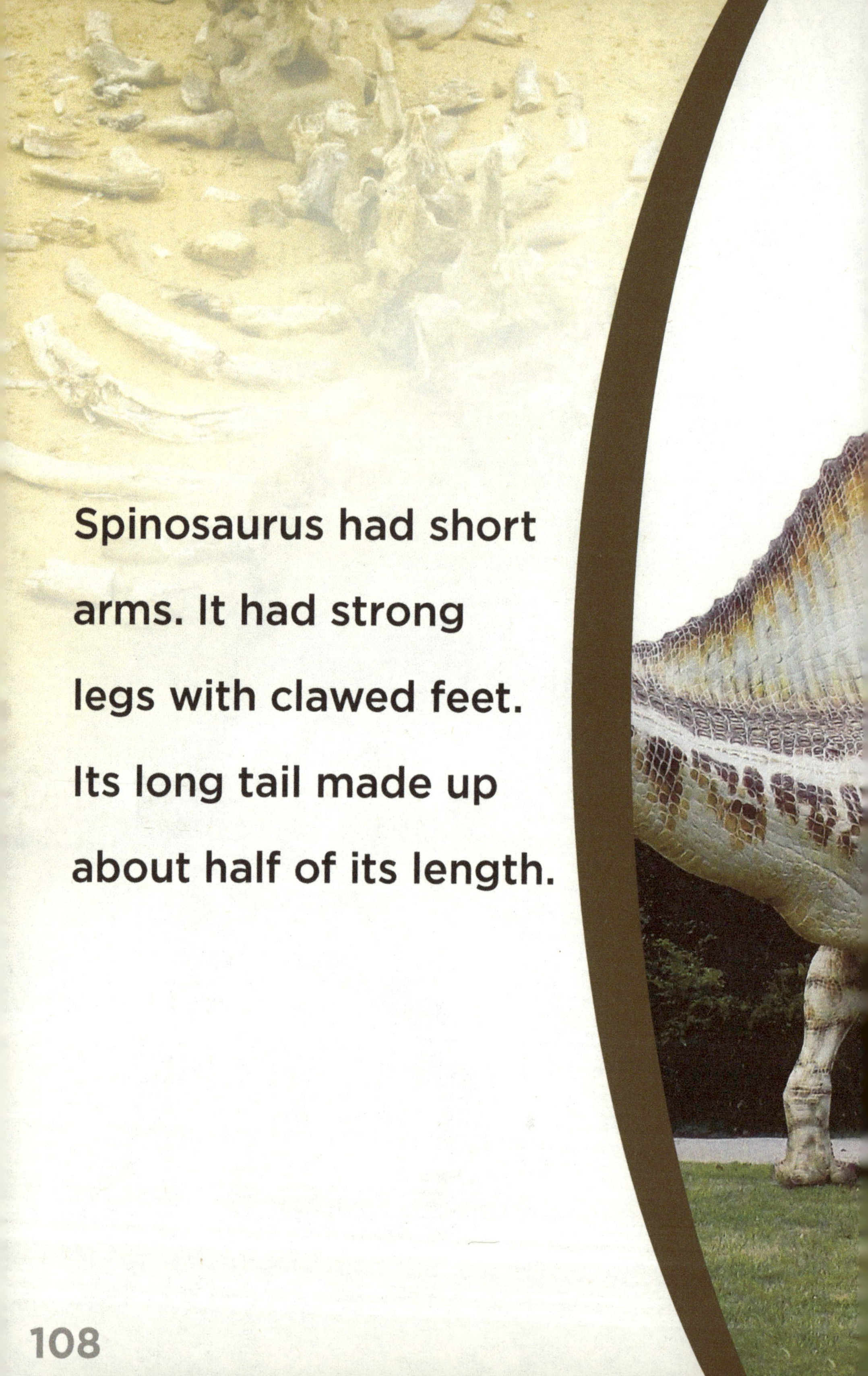

Spinosaurus had short arms. It had strong legs with clawed feet. Its long tail made up about half of its length.

Spinosaurus had
a long snout and
mouth. It looked like
a crocodile's mouth.
It also had lots of
long, pointed teeth.

Habitat &
Food

Spinosaurus spent
time in water and on
land. But it probably
moved much easier
in water. It ate lots of
large fish. It even ate
sharks!

Fossils

Spinosaurus fossils have been found in northern Africa. This area was filled with many bodies of water in the Cretaceous period. Today it is a large desert called the Sahara.

The first fossils were uncovered in Egypt in 1912. In 2008, a piece of finger bone and spine were found in Morocco.

Morocco
Egypt

More Facts

- The museum that held the most complete Spinosaurus remains was bombed in World War II. The fossils were destroyed.

- Spinosaurus had a snout filled with widely-spaced teeth. This was great for catching fish and other food.

- A Spinosaurus head was shaped much like a crocodile's. However, it was much larger at around 5 to 6 feet (1.5 to 1.8 m) long.

Glossary

Cretaceous period – rocks from the Cretaceous period often show early insects and the first flowering plants. The end of the Cretaceous period, about 65 million years ago, brought the mass extinction of dinosaurs.

fossil – the remains, impression, or trace of something that lived long ago, as a skeleton, footprint, etc.

sail – a broad, upright, and elongated spine that some dinosaurs had. It was likely used to control the body temperature of the dinosaur.

snout – the projecting nose and mouth of an animal.

theropod – a meat-eating dinosaur that came in many sizes and usually had small forelimbs.

Styracosaurus

by Grace Hansen

Table of Contents

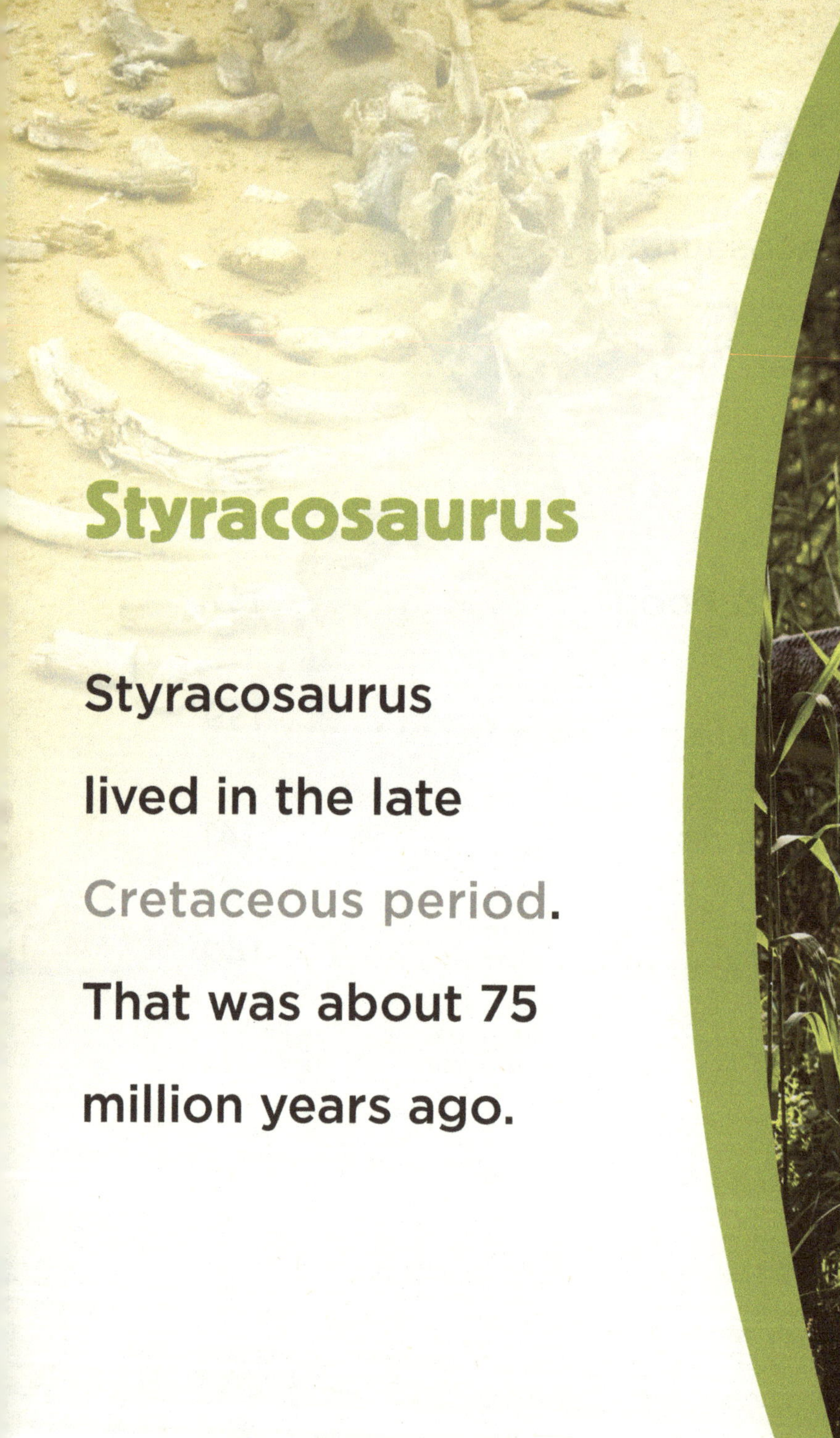

Styracosaurus

Styracosaurus

lived in the late

Cretaceous period.

That was about 75

million years ago.

Styracosaurus was

a ceratopsian. It

ate plants.

Habitat

North America looked very different when the Styracosaurus was alive. Much of the land was covered in a shallow sea. So this dinosaur lived near water.

Body

This dinosaur grew up to 18 feet (5.5 m) long. It weighed nearly 6,000 pounds (2,721.6 kg). It was about the same size as a rhinoceros.

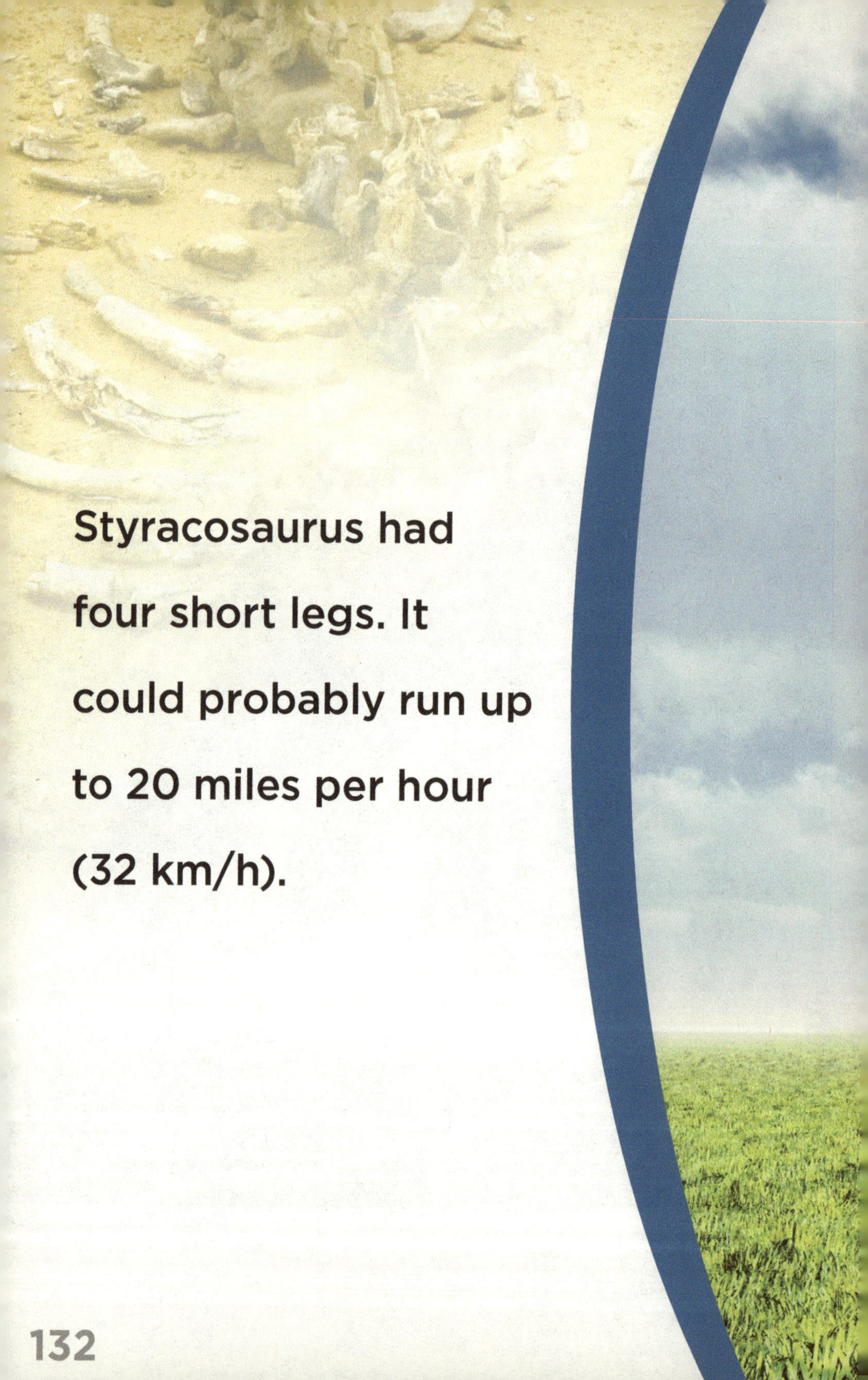

Styracosaurus had four short legs. It could probably run up to 20 miles per hour (32 km/h).

Styracosaurus is best known for its frill and horn. The frill was made of bone. It was very hard. Six long spikes grew out of it.

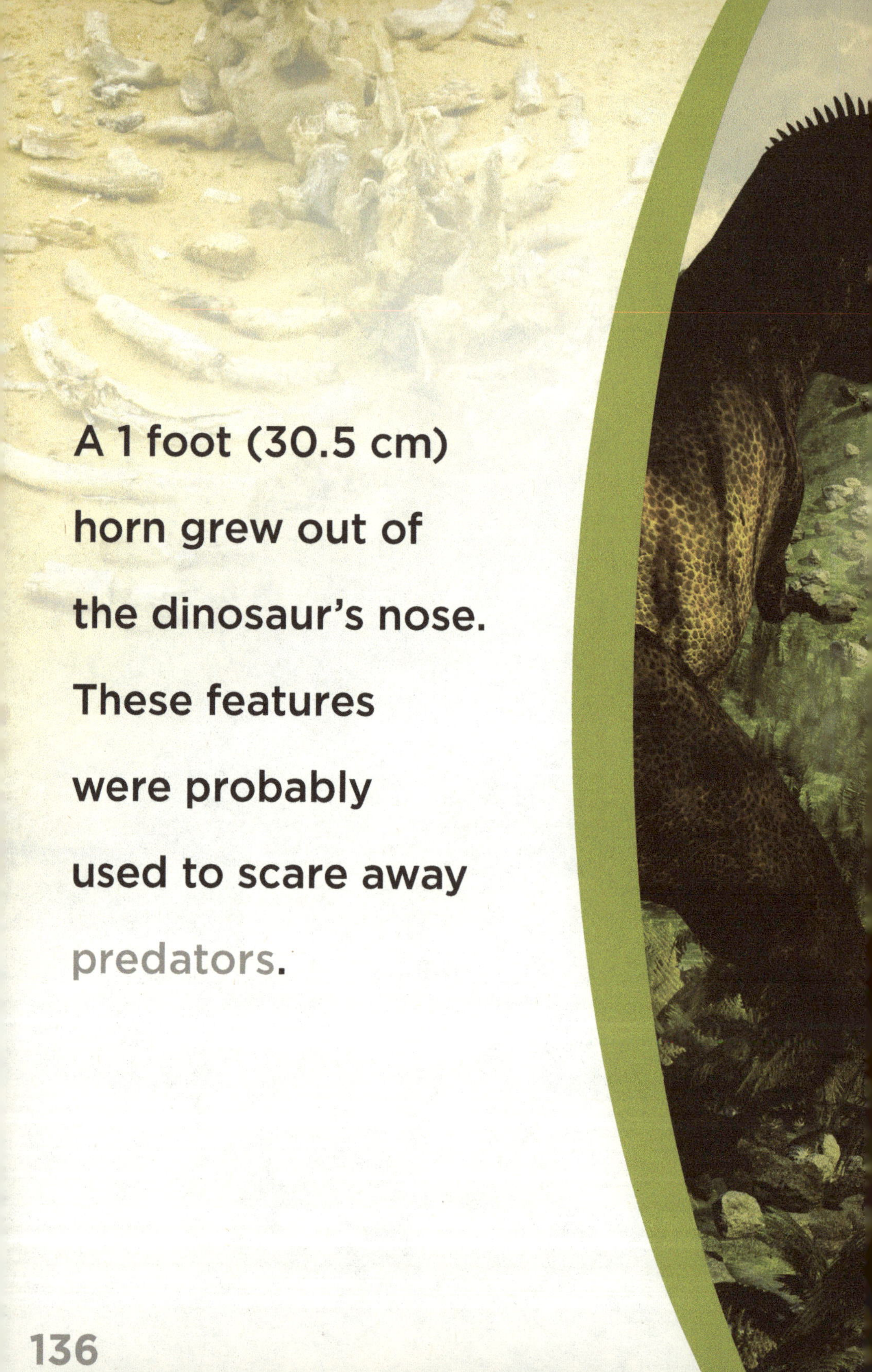

A 1 foot (30.5 cm) horn grew out of the dinosaur's nose. These features were probably used to scare away predators.

Eating & Food

The Styracosaurus had a beak. The beak helped tear leaves from plants. It also had teeth in the back of its mouth for chewing.

Fossils

This dinosaur probably lived in herds. Once, nearly 100 Styracosaurus fossils were found in one place. Fossils have been found in Montana and Alberta, Canada.

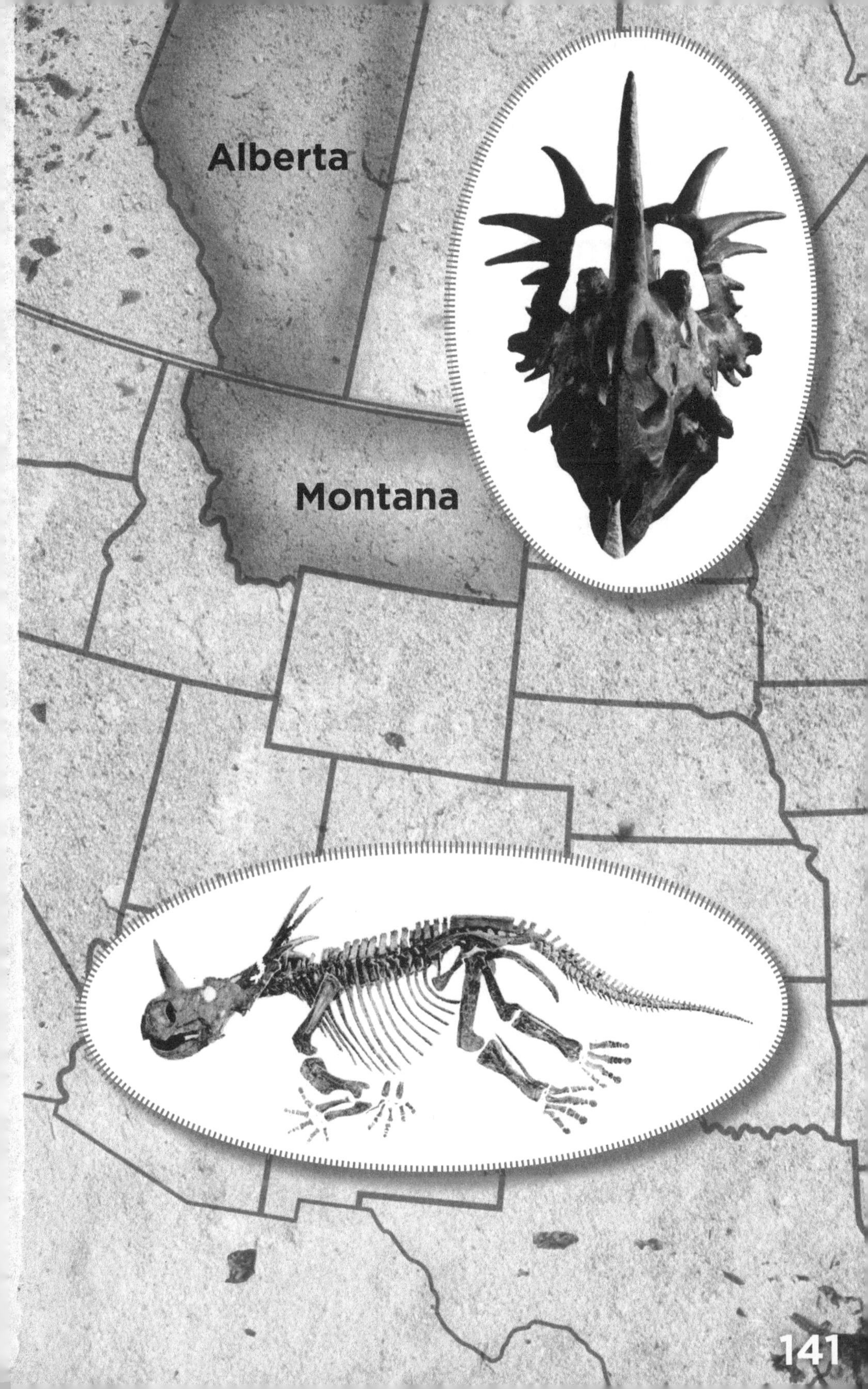

Alberta
Montana

More Facts

- The horn of a Styracosaurus was thought to have been around 20 inches (50.8 cm) long. But fossils have shown that the horn was more often around 10 inches (25.4 cm) long.

- When threatened, this dinosaur may have charged at its predators. This would have been a good defense!

- Living in a large herd was another way this dinosaur protected itself from predators.

Glossary

beak – the hard, pointed part of some dinosaurs' mouths.

ceratopsia – a group of beaked, plant-eating dinosaurs that lived in what are now North America, Europe, and Asia.

Cretaceous period – rocks from the Cretaceous period often show early insects and the first flowering plants. The end of the Cretaceous period, about 65 million years ago, brought the mass extinction of dinosaurs.

fossil – the remains, impression, or trace of something that lived long ago, as a skeleton, footprint, etc.

frill – a projection of bone from the neck of an animal.

predator – an animal that exists by hunting and eating other animals.

Carnotaurus

by Grace Hansen

Photo Credits: Alamy, iStock, Science Source, Shutterstock, Thinkstock, ©Ali Eminov p.9 / CC BY-NC 2.0, ©Dawn Pedersen p.19 / CC BY 2.0, ©Travail personnel p.21 / CC BY-SA 3.0

Production Contributors: Teddy Borth, Jennie Forsberg, Grace Hansen

Design Contributors: Dorothy Toth, Pakou Moua

Table of Contents

Carnotaurus

Carnotaurus was a large theropod. It lived during the late Cretaceous period. That was around 70 million years ago!

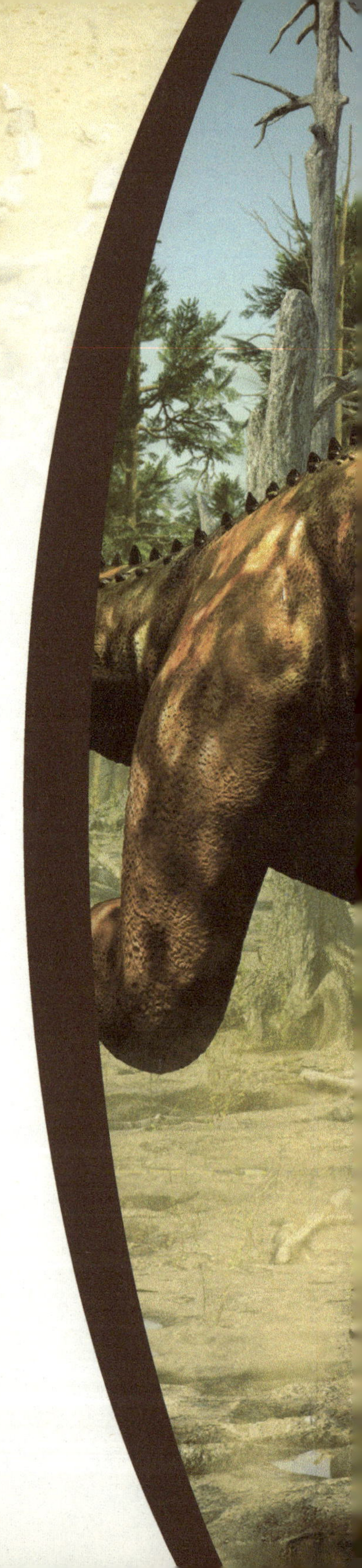

Habitat

Carnotaurus lived in what is South America today. It dwelled in wetlands and plains near the coast.

Body

Carnotaurus was around 30 feet (9.1 m) long. It weighed between 2,000 and 3,000 pounds (900 to 1,400 kg).

It had very tiny,
useless arms for its
large body. Its small
fingers did not work.

Carnotaurus had large, powerful legs. Its tail was about 13 feet (3.96 m) long and helped it balance. Its legs and tail helped it run quickly.

Carnotaurus had horns above its eyes. The horns were about 6 inches (15.24 cm) long. They were likely used for fighting or hunting.

Food

Carnotaurus means "meat-eating bull." It lived among much smaller animals. It was an apex predator in its habitat.

Fossils

José Bonaparte discovered and named the Carnotaurus. Bonaparte was a famous paleontologist.

The first fossil was unearthed in Argentina in 1984. Bonaparte found an almost complete Carnotaurus skeleton.

North America
South America
Argentina

More Facts

- Carnotaurus did not give big blows to each other with their horns. Instead, they likely pushed up against each other using the sides of their skulls.

- Carnotaurus used quick bites to catch prey. This is because its usual prey was small and fast.

- Carnotaurus was one of the fastest animals during the time it lived.

Glossary

apex predator – the top predator of a food chain that has no natural predators.

Cretaceous period – A period of geological time that began 145 million years ago. The end of the Cretaceous period, about 66 million years ago, brought the mass extinction of dinosaurs.

fossil – the remains, impression, or trace of something that lived long ago, as a skeleton, footprint, etc.

paleontologist – a scientist that studies paleontology, the science that studies animal and plant fossils for information about life in the past.

theropod – any dinosaur of the suborder Theropoda, such as Tyrannosaurus rex and velociraptor, characterized by hollow bones and three-toed limbs, usually possessing short forelimbs and walking on two legs.

Gastornis

by Grace Hansen

Photo Credits: Alamy, iStock, Science Source, Shutterstock, Thinkstock, ©Vince Smith p.21 / CC BY-SA 2.0

Production Contributors: Teddy Dorth, Jennie Forsberg, Grace Hansen

Design Contributors: Dorothy Toth, Pakou Moua

Table of Contents

Gastornis

Gastornis was a large bird. It lived around 56 million years ago during the Cenozoic era.

Habitat

Gastornis lived in tropical areas. It could be found roaming rain forests.

Body

Gastornis was a huge bird! It stood at least 6 feet (1.8 m) tall on two thick legs.

Gastornis's body
was strong and
heavy. It was
covered in feathers.

Even though Gastornis was a bird, it could not fly. Its tiny wings were useless.

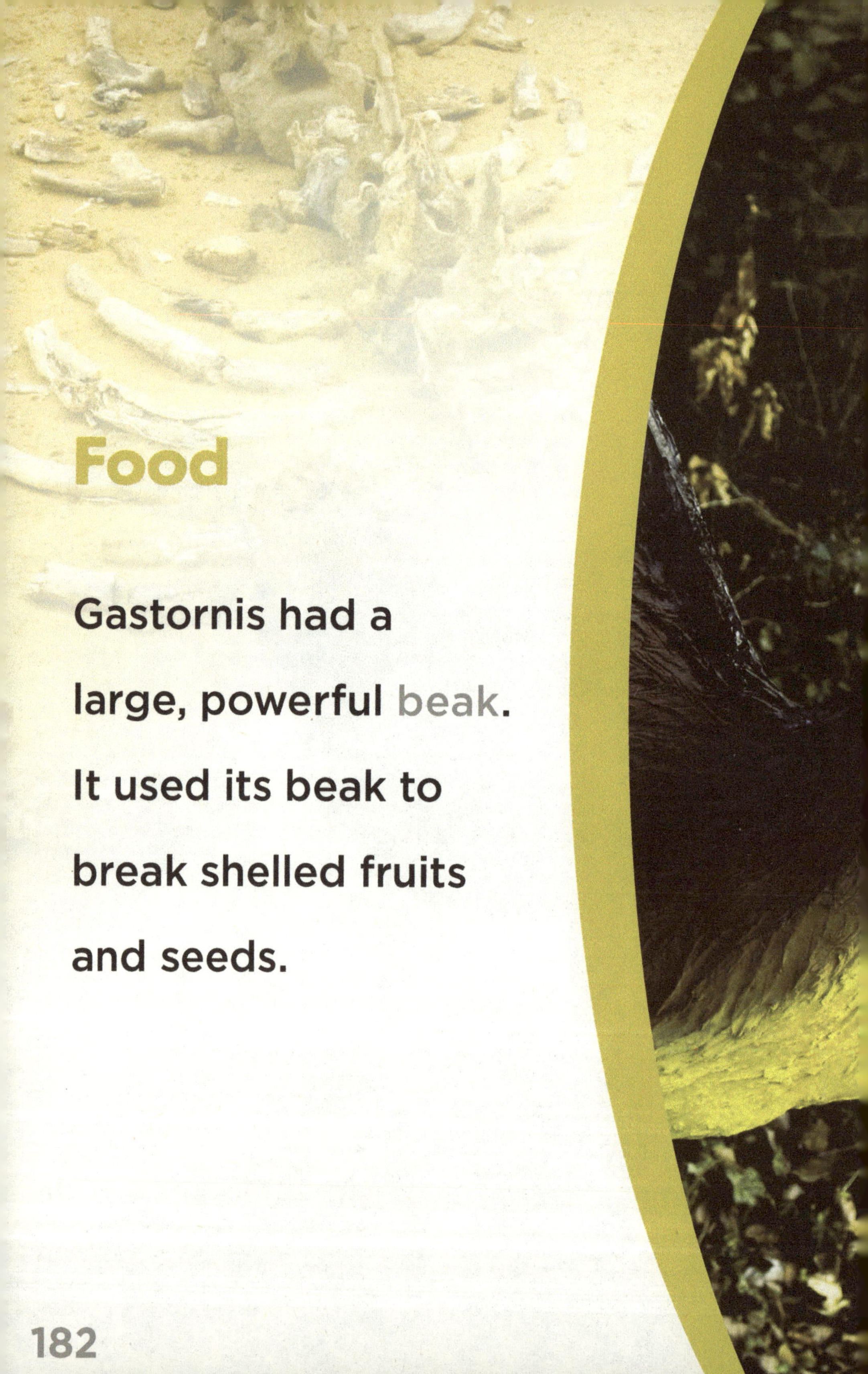

Food

Gastornis had a large, powerful beak. It used its beak to break shelled fruits and seeds.

Scientists once thought it was a meat-eater. But they have now learned the bird was a herbivore.

Fossils

Gaston Planté found the first Gastornis fossils. He was a French scientist. In 1855, the prehistoric bird was named after its discoverer. Its name means "Gaston's bird."

Gaston Planté

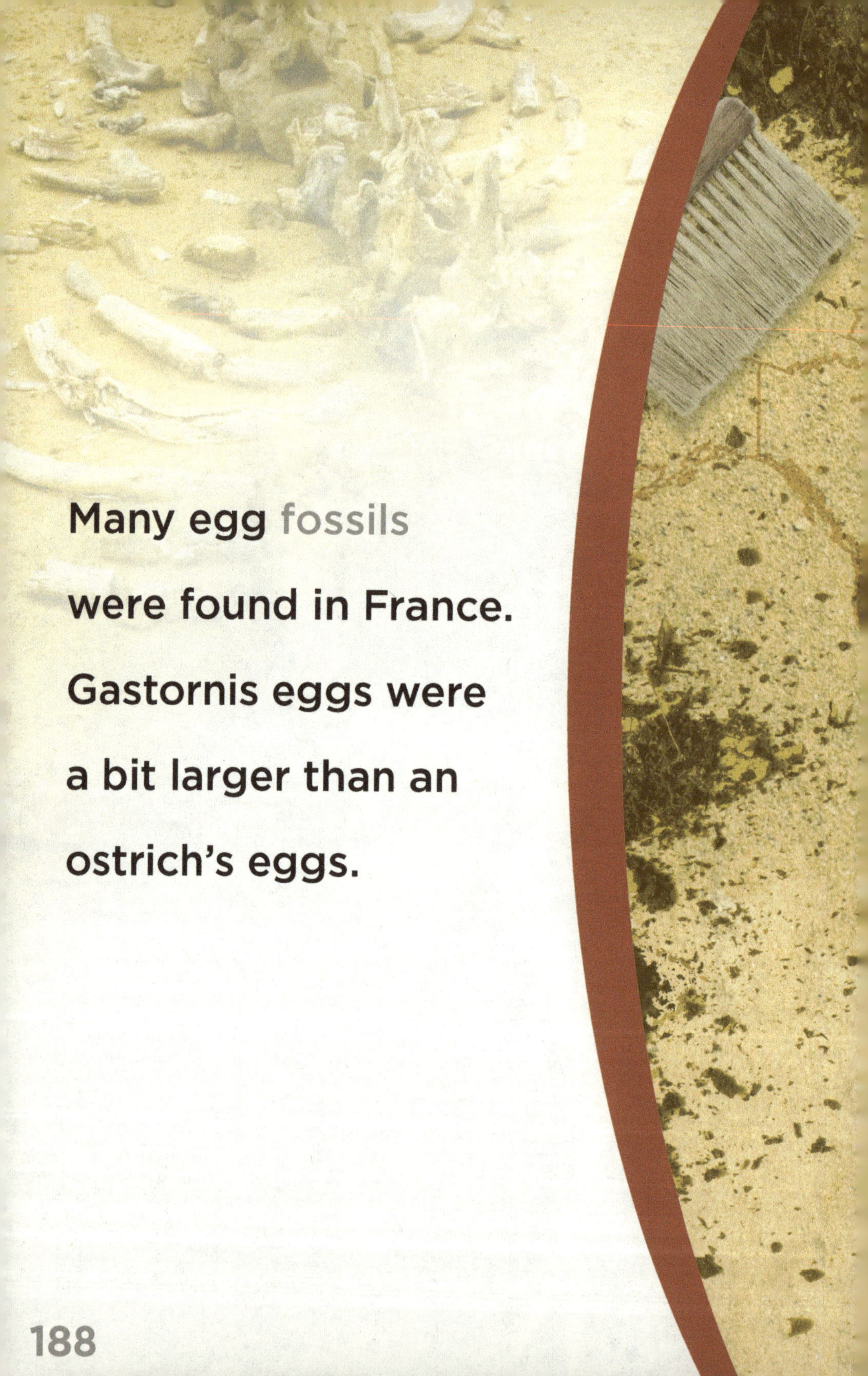

Many egg fossils
were found in France.
Gastornis eggs were
a bit larger than an
ostrich's eggs.

United States
France

More Facts

- Gastornis likely weighed around 400 pounds (181 kg).

- Scientists learned about what Gastornis ate from its remains. Its remains showed no evidence that the large bird ate meat.

- Another clue that Gastornis was a herbivore came from its beak. Though it was large and powerful, it did not have a hook at the end. Beaks made for meat-eating usually have a hooked tip.

Glossary

beak – the hard-pointed part of some dinosaurs' mouths.

Cenozoic Era – the third of the major eras of Earth's history, beginning about 65 million years ago extending to the present. It began after the mass extinction event that ended the Cretaceous period.

fossil – the remains, impression, or trace of something that lived long ago, as a skeleton, footprint, etc.

herbivore – an animal that only feeds on plants.

prehistoric – belonging to a period in a time before written history.

Mosasaurus

by Grace Hansen

Table of Contents

Mosasaurus

Mosasaurus was not an actual dinosaur. It was a marine reptile.

It lived in the late

Cretaceous period.

This was about 70

million years ago.

Habitat

Mosasaurus ruled the prehistoric seas. It mostly lived in what is the North Atlantic Ocean today.

It lived near the water's surface. Mosasaurus did this because it breathed air.

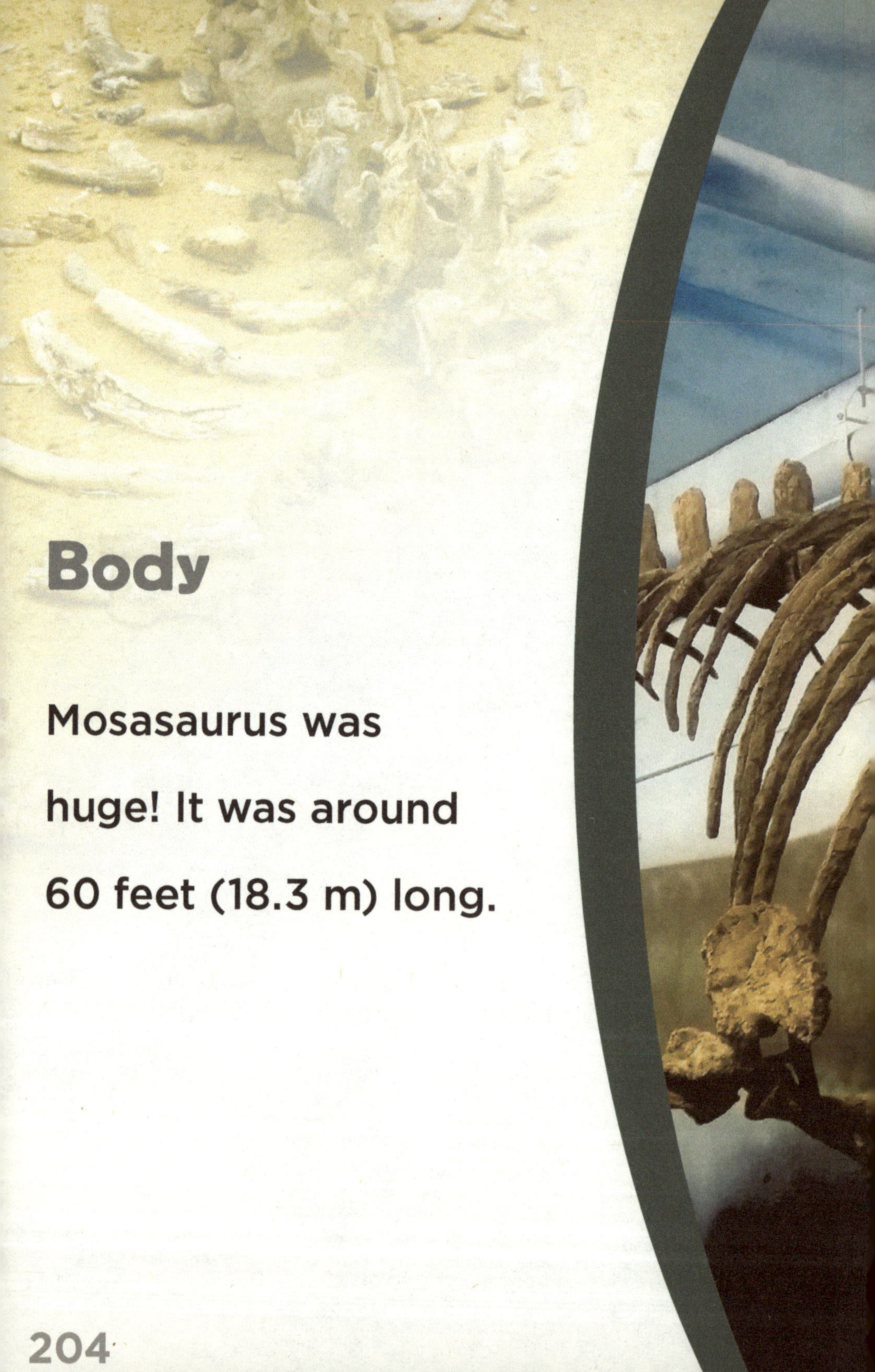

Body

Mosasaurus was huge! It was around 60 feet (18.3 m) long.

It had two sets of fins.

Its tail was large and

powerful.

Mosasaurus's giant
head was filled
with sharp teeth.
Its teeth helped it
catch its prey.

Food

Mosasaurus was not a picky eater. Its diet included fish, birds, and anything else that came in its path.

Fossils

The first Mosasaur remains found were pieces of a skull. The fossils were dug up in 1764 near the Meuse River in the Netherlands. Mosasaurus means "Lizard of the Meuse River."

Netherlands
France

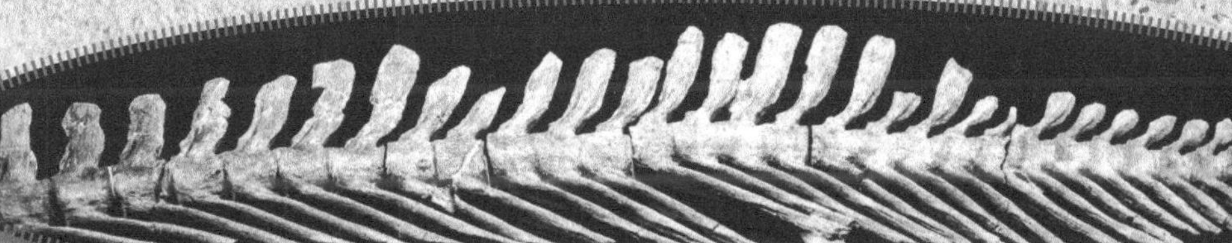

More Facts

- Mosasaurus is part of the Mosasaur family. There are nearly 38 types of Mosasaurs. All of them were marine reptiles that breathed air.

- All Mosasaurs had double-hinged jaws. This is how they opened their mouths so wide.

- Mosasaurus fossils have also been found in the United States, Canada, Africa, Japan, and many more countries.

Glossary

Cretaceous period – A period of geological time that began 145 million years ago. The end of the Cretaceous period, about 66 million years ago, brought the mass extinction of dinosaurs.

fossil – the remains, impression, or trace of something that lived long ago, as a skeleton, footprint, etc.

marine reptile – a reptile that is adapted to live in the sea.

prehistoric – belonging to a period in a time before written history.

prey – an animal hunted and eaten by another animal.

Parasaurolophus

by Grace Hansen

Table of Contents

Parasaurolophus

Parasaurolophus lived during the late Cretaceous period. That was around 75 million years ago. This dinosaur roamed land that is now North America.

Body

Parasaurolophus was about 32 feet (10 m) long from head to tail. It weighed around 8,000 pounds (3,628 kg).

Parasaurolophus (PAIR-uh-sor-AH-luh-fus)
is an ornithopod dinosaur
"Duck-billed" hadrosaurs had beaks, not bills
Parasaurolophus is a hadrosaur, a diverse group of ornithopods commonly known as "duck-billed" dinosaurs. But the nickname is misleading. The hadrosaur "bill" was nothing like a duck's toothless bill. At the front, a horny beak cropped bites of tough plant material. Hundreds of teeth then ground the leafy bite to a pulp.
against one another in a forward-and-backward chewing motion, the hundreds of teeth in a hadrosaur's mouth made short work of tough plant matter. As old teeth wore out, new ones grew in.

Its head alone was around 6 feet (1.8 m) long. This included a large crest that the dinosaur is known for.

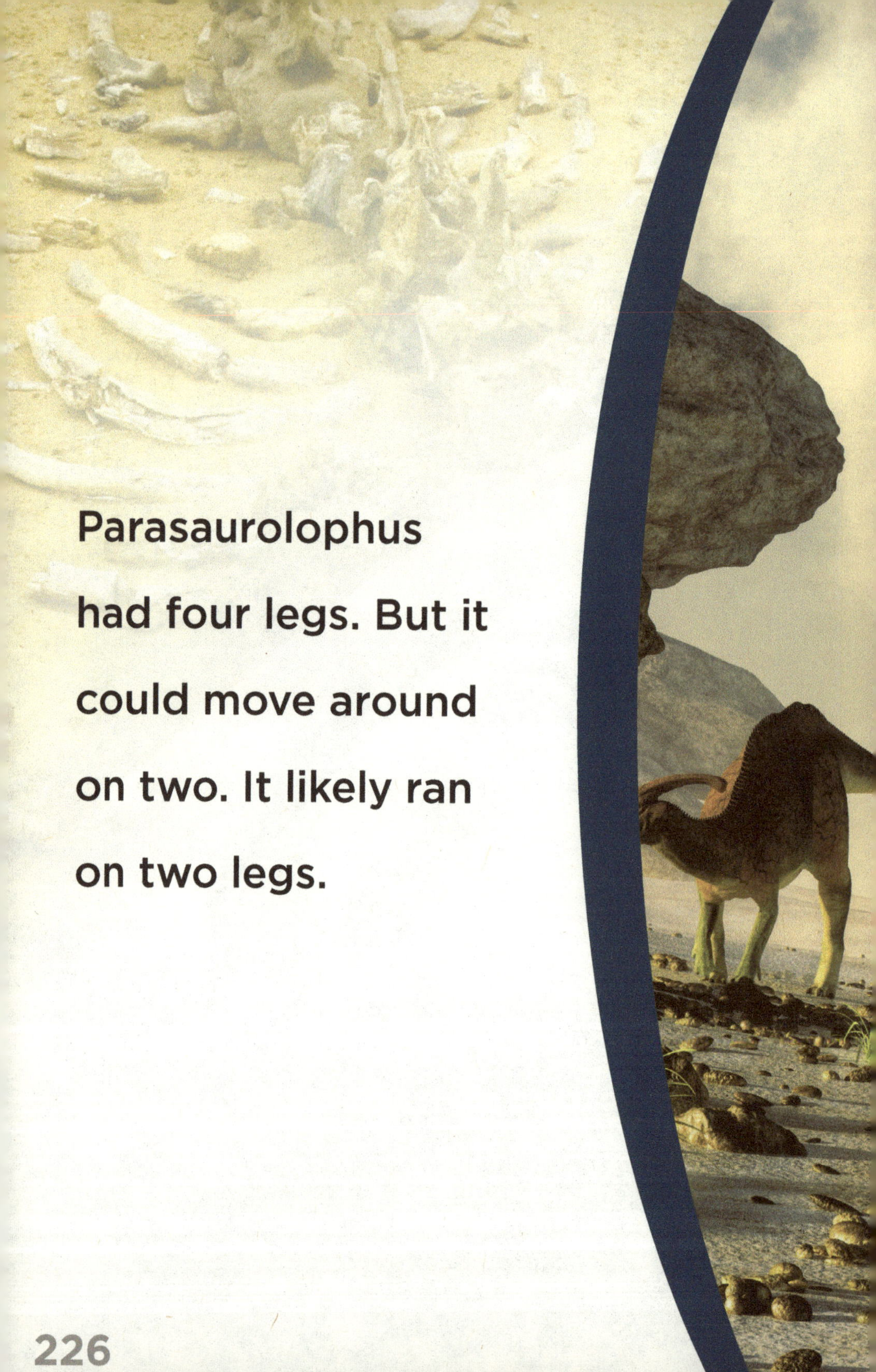

Parasaurolophus had four legs. But it could move around on two. It likely ran on two legs.

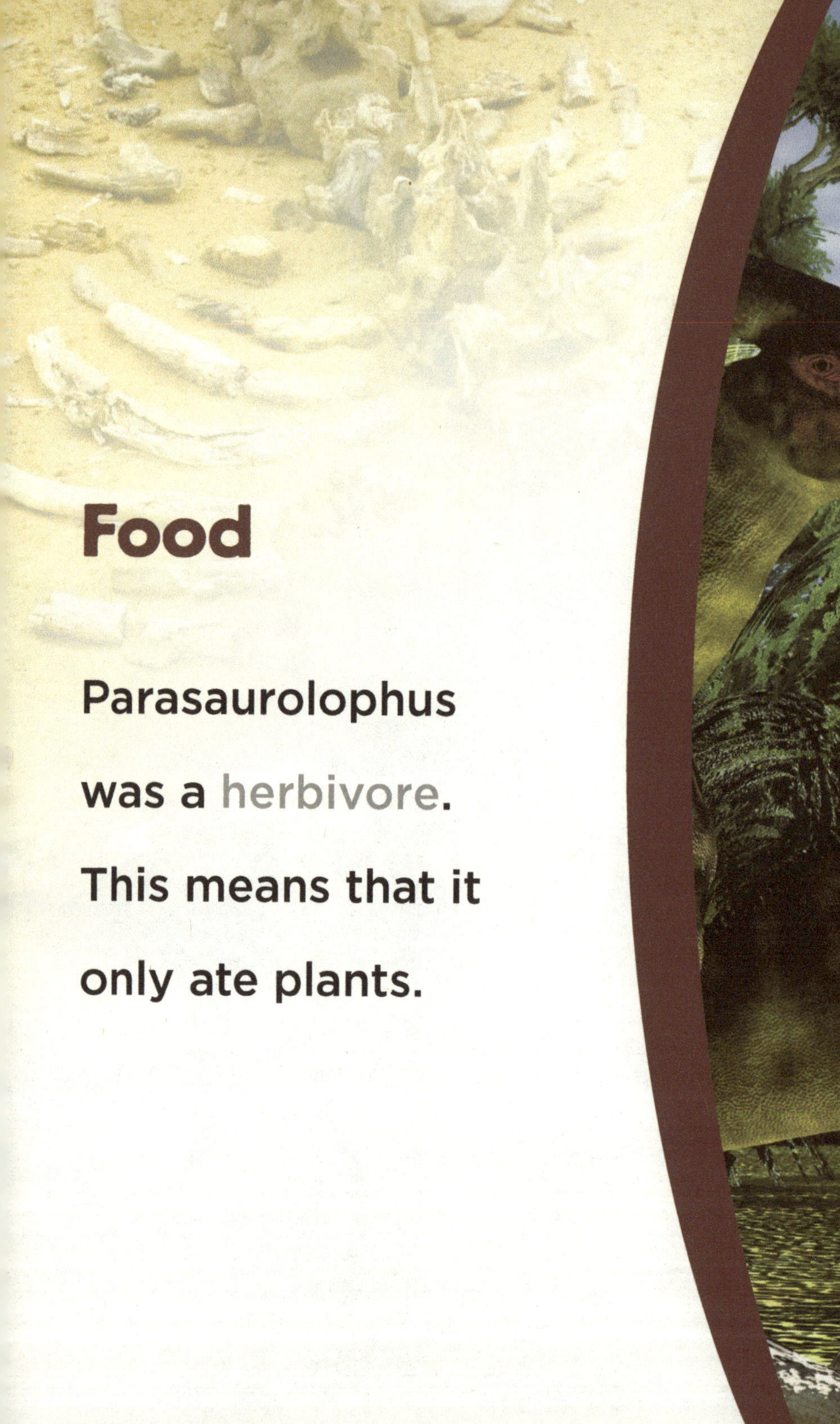

Food

Parasaurolophus
was a herbivore.
This means that it
only ate plants.

It plucked plants with
its bill-like mouth. It
chewed up the plants
in a grinding motion.

The grinding would wear down the dinosaur's teeth. New teeth would replace old ones.

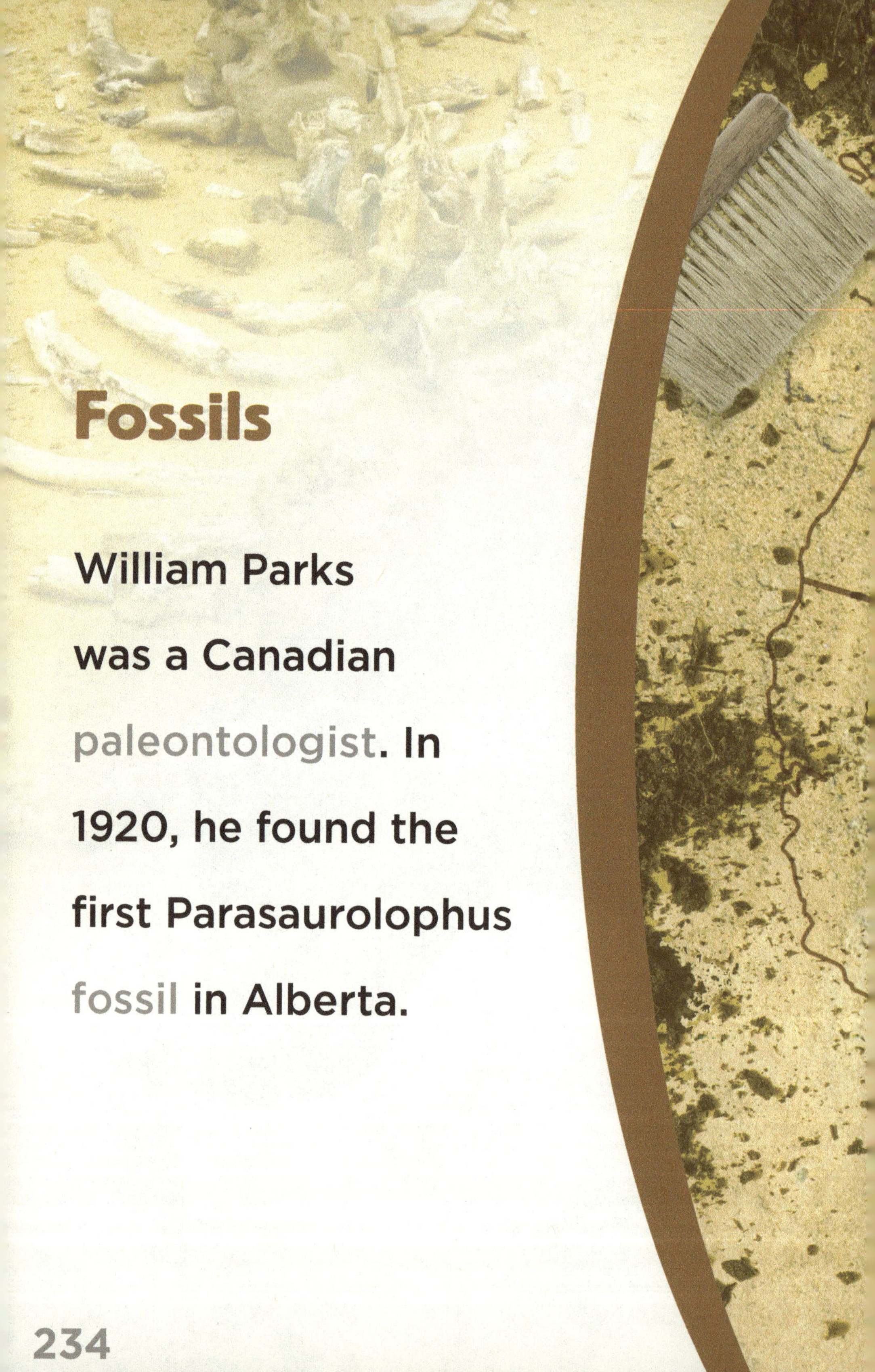

Fossils

William Parks was a Canadian paleontologist. In 1920, he found the first Parasaurolophus fossil in Alberta.

235

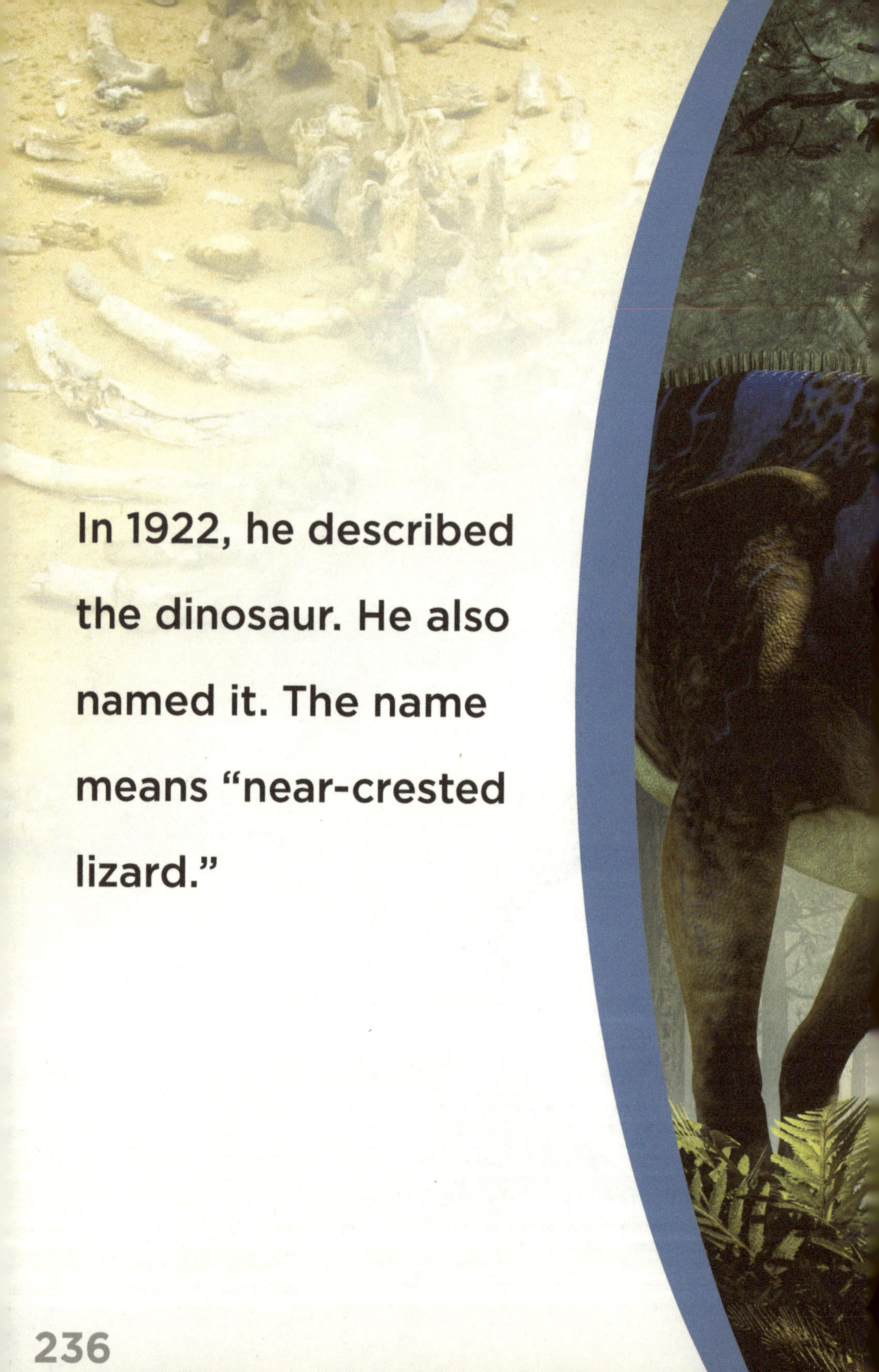

In 1922, he described the dinosaur. He also named it. The name means "near-crested lizard."

More Facts

- Parasaurolophus fossils have also been found in Utah and New Mexico.

- Scientists think the dinosaur might have used its crest to make a loud sound. It would use this sound to talk to other Parasaurolophus.

- This dinosaur was covered in small scales.

Glossary

crest – a tuft of feathers or bone on an animal's head.

Cretaceous period – a period of geological time that began 145 million years ago. The end of the Cretaceous period, about 66 million years ago, brought the mass extinction of the dinosaurs.

fossil – the remains, impression, or trace of something that lived long ago, as a skeleton, footprint, etc.

herbivore – an animal that only feeds on plants.

paleontologist – a scientist that studies paleontology, the science that studies animal and plant fossils for information about life in the past.

Plesiosaurus

by Grace Hansen

Table of Contents

Plesiosaurus

Plesiosaurus lived
during the early
Jurassic period.
That was around 190
million years ago.

Plesiosaurus was not a dinosaur. It was a marine reptile. It was just one of a few kinds of plesiosaur.

Habitat

It swam in waters that surrounded what is the United Kingdom today.

Body

Plesiosaurus was a smaller plesiosaur. It grew to be about 10 to 15 feet (3-4.5 m) long. It weighed around 2,000 pounds (907 kg).

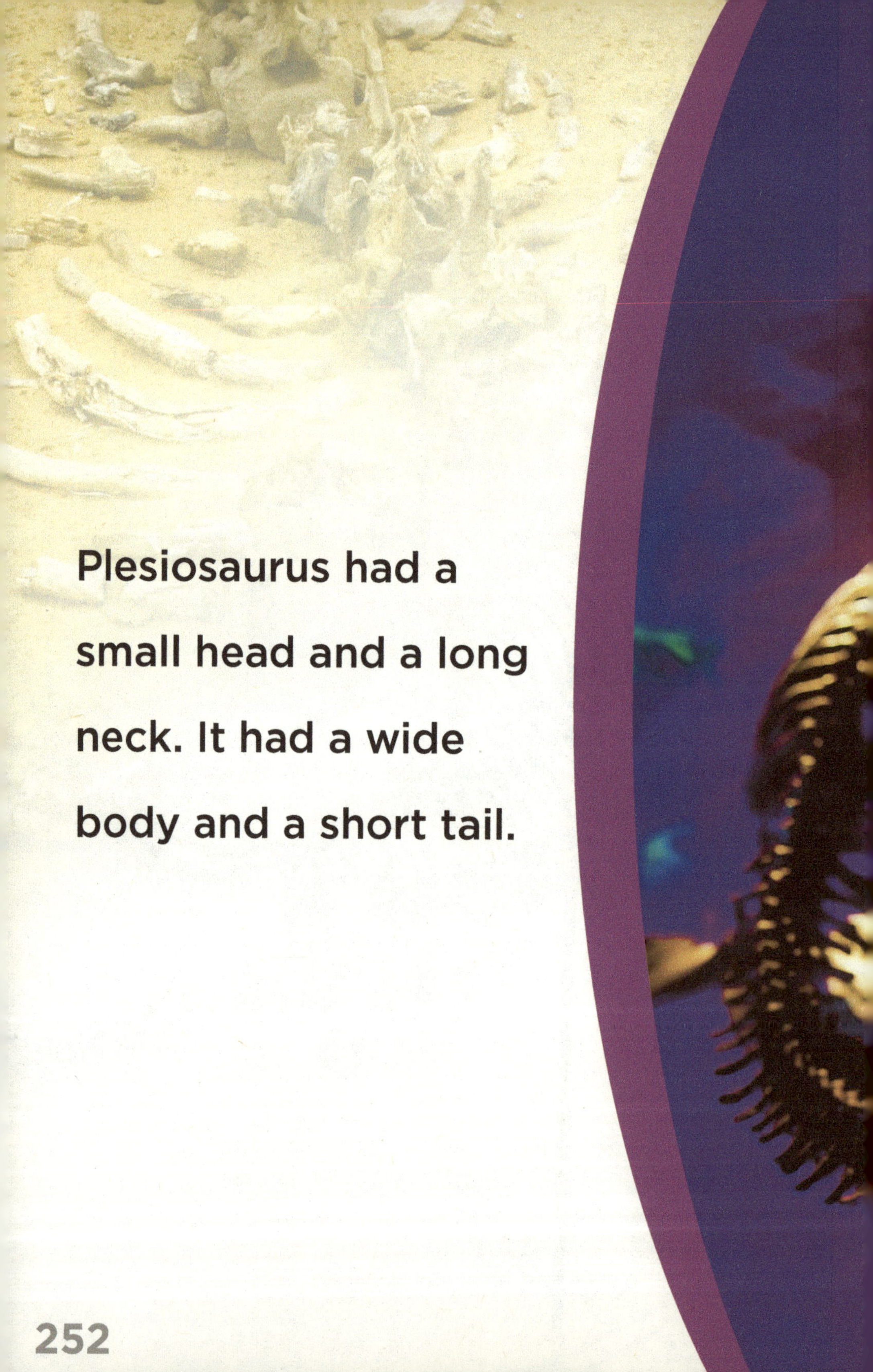

Plesiosaurus had a small head and a long neck. It had a wide body and a short tail.

Plesiosaurus had four large flippers that moved it through the water. It stayed near the water's surface. This is because it breathed air.

Food

This reptile was a carnivore. It had sharp teeth to catch its prey. It ate lots of different things, like belemnites and fish.

Fossils

An almost-perfect
Plesiosaurus skeleton
was found in 1823.
English paleontologist
Mary Anning
uncovered it.

Mary Anning

Anning dug up the
fossils near Dorset,
England. Plesiosaurus
had earned its name
a few years earlier. It
means "near lizard."

Europe

England

Dorset

More Facts

- Plesiosaurus would hunt by swimming through large groups of fish. It had needle-like teeth that were good at catching fish!

- Even though Plesiosaurus was not a dinosaur, it still lived at the same time the dinosaurs did.

- Plesiosaurus had smooth skin to help it swim easily through water.

Glossary

belemnite – an extinct kind of mollusk that is typically found as a fossil in marine deposits of the Jurassic and Cretaceous periods.

carnivore – an animal that only eats meat.

fossil – the remains, impression, or trace of something that lived long ago, as a skeleton, footprint, etc.

Jurassic period – a geological period that lasted 56 million years until the beginning of the Cretaceous period.

marine reptile – a reptile that lives in the water.

paleontologist – a scientist that studies paleontology, the science that studies animal and plant fossils for information about life in the past.

plesiosaur – a large extinct marine reptile with a broad body, large paddle-like limbs, and typically a long and flexible neck and small head.

Pterodactyl

by Grace Hansen

Table of Contents

Pterodactyl

Pterodactyl lived during the late Jurassic period. This was about 150 million years ago.

It was a kind of
pterosaur. Pterosaurs
are not dinosaurs.
They are flying
reptiles.

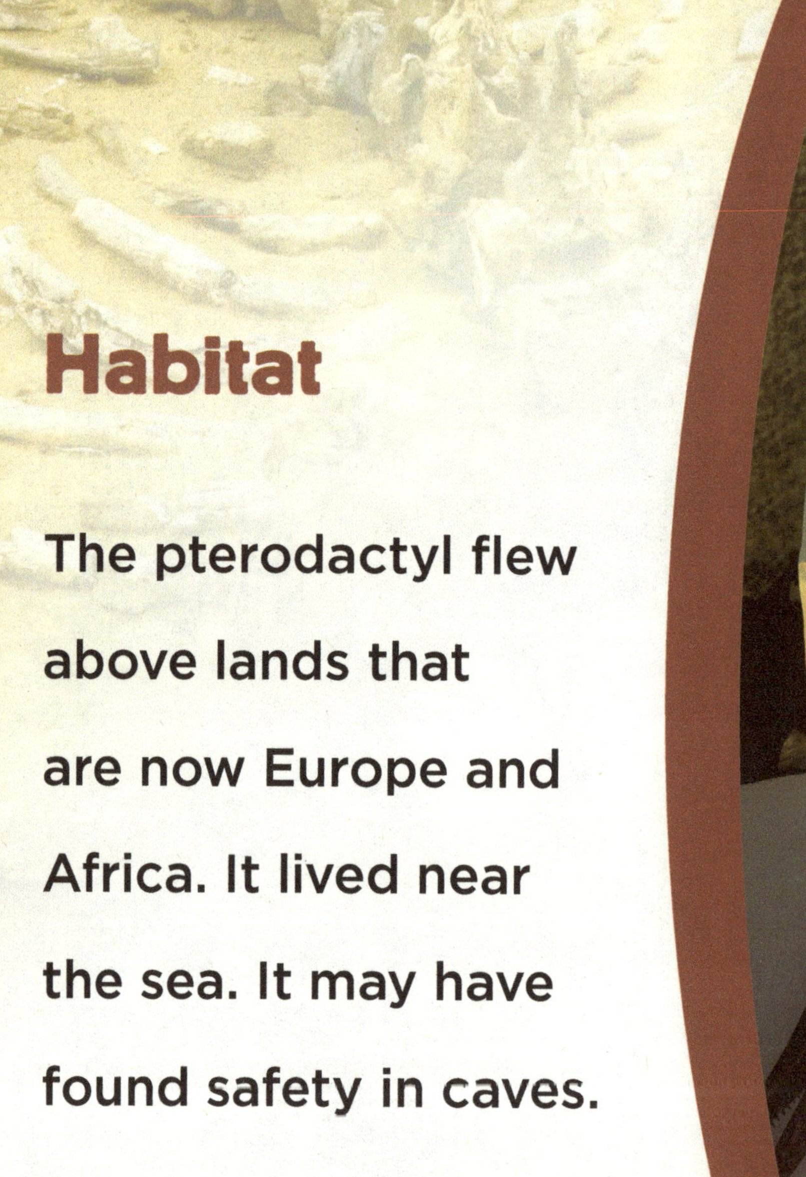

Habitat

The pterodactyl flew above lands that are now Europe and Africa. It lived near the sea. It may have found safety in caves.

Body

Pterodactyl is a nickname for *pterodactylus*, which means "winged finger." It was named this because of its extra-long fourth fingers. The wings stretched from these fingers to its legs.

Pterodactyl was about 3.5 feet (1.1 m) long. It likely only weighed around 10 pounds (4.5 kg). This was small compared to other pterosaurs.

Pterodactyl pushed
off the ground with
its feet. Then it
flapped its wings
to gain height
and speed.

Its wingspan was around 3.6 feet (1.1 m) long. It spent most of its time gliding through the air.

Food

Pterodactyl had a long beak. The beak was filled with sharp teeth to catch prey. Pterodactyl was a carnivore that liked to eat fish, eggs, and small animals.

Fossils

Pterodactyl was the first pterosaur to be identified. The first fossils were found in Bavaria, Germany, in 1784. Since then, more remains have been found in Europe and Africa.

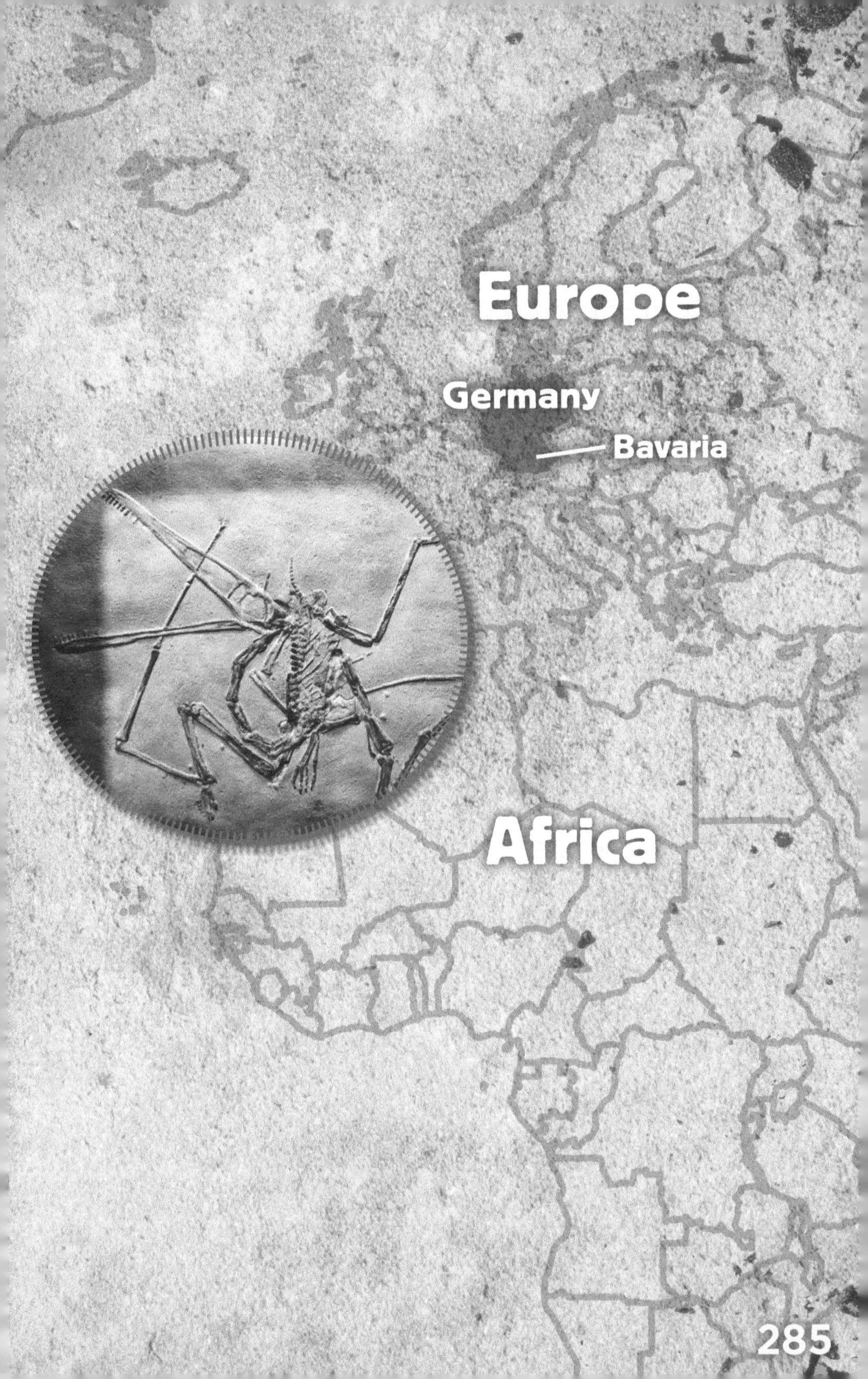

Europe
Germany
Bavaria
Africa

More Facts

- Scientists believe there is only one species of pterodactylus. Its scientific name is *Pterodactylus antiquus*.

- Italian scientist Cosimo Collini was the first person to find pterodactyl fossils. He thought he had found fossils from a marine animal. It was later learned that the remains belonged to a flying creature.

- Pterodactyl had about 90 razor sharp teeth!

Glossary

carnivore – an animal that only eats meat.

glide – to move smoothly and continuously along without effort.

Jurassic period – a geological period that lasted 56 million years until the beginning of the Cretaceous period.

prey – an animal hunted and eaten by another animal.

reptile – a cold-blooded animal with a skeleton inside its body and dry scales or hard plates on its skin.

wingspan – the distance from the tip of one wing of a flying animal to the tip of the other wing.